NOTES

OF A

METALLURGICAL JOURNEY

IN EUROPE.

BY

JOHN A. CHURCH,

ENGINEER OF MINES.

WITH TWENTY-TWO ILLUSTRATIONS.

NEW YORK:
D. VAN NOSTRAND, PUBLISHER,
23 MURRAY AND 27 WARREN STREET.
1873.

TO

THOMAS EGLESTON, JR.,

PROFESSOR OF MINERALOGY AND METALLURGY IN THE SCHOOL OF MINES, COLUMBIA COLLEGE, NEW YORK,

THIS VOLUME IS RESPECTFULLY INSCRIBED.

INDEX.

PREFACE.

The Notes which form the basis of the few papers that make up this book were taken solely for private use, and there was no intention of making them public until after the lapse of a considerable time. Their publication was then undertaken, not because they presented descriptions of novel processes, but because the author found that the poverty of English technical literature in this branch of industry was such as to be a serious annoyance to men engaged in the treatment of American ores. They first appeared in the columns of the Engineering and Mining Journal, and their reception has been sufficiently favorable to warrant this republication.

It is frequently said that American genius can be trusted to devise its own processes and need not go abroad for instruction, but no one who is acquainted with the industry, skill and devotion of European metallurgists to their work can be willing to lose the fruits of their experiment and thought. Few persons know how much labor and money are spent by them every year in the work of revising old established processes, both by laboratory examination and by experiments conducted on the largest scale. The two years that elapsed between the author's journey in Europe and the publication of these Notes was sufficient to bring about such changes and improvements in foreign practice that he could no longer rely upon the details of his work but was obliged to collate it with the latest technical publications abroad. He is therefore indebted to many writers and has endeavored to properly express this fact in foot notes to each paper. But he has not described any works that were not visited and carefully studied by him, and trusts that the personal knowledge thus gained has enabled him to appropriate with success and incorporate with his own, the work of others.

NOTES

ON A

METALLURGICAL JOURNEY IN EUROPE.

The Copper Process at Agordo

AGORDO is reached from Venice by rail to Conegliano, stage to Belluno and post-chaise to Agordo, the whole journey occupying about eighteen hours. The old process in use at this place has been fully described by RIVOT, in his work on Metallurgy ; by HATON, in the *Annales des Mines*, 1855, 5th series, vol. 8 ; by PERCY, in his metallurgy, and many other writers. It will, therefore, receive only such attention here as is necessary to make the character of the recent changes sufficiently clear.

The ore is obtained from an irregular deposit of iron pyrites, lying in black argillaceous schist, close to the contact plane of a dolomite limestone. The dimensions allotted to this mass by Engineer PELLATI, are :

Length	550 meters.
Breadth	35 "
Depth	200 "
Contents in cubic meters	1,764,000

He reports the state of the work in 1865, as follows :[1]

Content of mass, cubic meters		1,764,000
Already excavated	"	617,000
Worthless pyrites	"	441,000
Good ore remaining	"	700,000

As the weight of one cubic meter of pyrites is 4,250 k. (9,350 lbs.) we have about 3,000,000,000 kilograms, or 3,000,000 tons. The present production is about 20,000 tons a year, at which rate the mine will hold out a hundred and fifty years.

About one-third of the ore (see above statement) is worthless, containing no copper. This is sorted out, and the remainder is separated into the following varieties :

Best ore....with 4 per cent. copper.
Good ore...with 2—4 per cent. copper.
Poor ore....with 0·4—2 per cent. copper.
Small ore...with 1—2 per cent. copper.

---

1. For information contained in these notes on Agordo, I am indebted to SIGNOR N. PELLATI, Engineer in charge for the Italian Government ; and to SIGNOR LUIGI HUBERT. Director of the Smelting Works.

This small ore is composed of a mixture of all the other varieties, and also of ore from a particular layer in the mine. It forms somewhat more than 15 per cent. of the whole.

Besides the pyrites a small amount of galena mixed with blende and containing a variable percentage of silver, is obtained. At the time of my visit, a gentleman had purchased a few hundred tons of this ore and was roasting it in piles, in the hope that the blende would roast to sulphate and thus be soluble. It has been ascertained that when a mixture of lead, zinc and silver sulphides are roasted together to sulphates, the silver is not soluble in the presence of so much lead. His roasting, therefore, had for its object the removal of the zinc and the concentration of the silver in the lead; but I have never been able to ascertain what success he had, though I am under the impression that his experiment failed.

In treating this mass, remarkable for its purity, methods were adopted which made Agordo the study of scientific men. The ore was roasted in heaps containing 250 to 300 tons, the temperature being kept very low, and after six to nine months, when the pile was opened, a kernel of unroasted ore was found in each lump. In this kernel was concentrated most of the copper which in the beginning had been distributed throughout the lump. A transmission of solid matter so remarkable as this, illustrating the operations by which metallic matter may be concentrated in veins by mundane fires, could not fail to attract attention, and nearly all writers on the metallurgy of copper, and processes of roasting, have discussed it.[2] These kernels were broken from the surrounding "shells," and in this way kernels of a working average of 4—8 per cent. copper were obtained from ore containing 2 per cent. and less; while the shells would contain about 0·7 per cent. The concentration of copper is so perfect that the real kernel often contains 30 per cent., but in order to make sure that none of the rich kernel shall be lost, a large quantity of shell is left around it, so that the working average is that above given.

Sulphur is collected in small depressions, stamped in the top of the pile. Fine, sifted ore, from the lixiviation vats, is stamped into circular basins and a small quantity of sulphur, from one-fifth to one-half of one per cent. of the ores' weight, collects in them. This is refined in the usual way. It contains arsenic and is not a very valuable product. In 1865 the amount made was 50,532 k. or 50·5 tons. This is 0·3 per cent. of the ore or 0·6 per cent. of the sulphur in the ore.

The treament of the two sorts was: Lixiviation of the shells with precipitation of the copper by iron, and fusion of the kernels.

THE WET TREATMENT.

Lixiviation. The ore is shovelled into vats 50 × 3·50 meters square and 1·50 meters deep; charge 14 tons. Fresh ore is lixiviated with liquor which has already served for two lixiviations, and in this way it is brought up to the proper strength. The liquor remains 24 hours in contact with the ore, is then drawn off, and the ore shovelled to a fresh tank, where it is treated with water from a

---

2. See Plattner's Röst Prozesse.

previous third lixiviation. After 24 hours standing the process is repeated, this time with fresh water. After the third contact with the ore, the liquor marks 32° BEAUME. Liquor from the second lixiviation marks 13°—14° B. The spent ore is placed on and under a new roasting heap, where the sulphurous acid fumes effect a re-roasting of it. It is then washed in 4 waters, sifted through a mesh of 1·5 centimeters = 0·6 inch, and the coarse ore receives a third treatment in the piles.

Cementation. The liquor from the lixiviation vats is clarified by settling in tanks, and then run to the cementation vats. These are of two kinds: lead tanks 4 × 3 meters and 1·5 meter deep, containing 21 cubic meters. They are heated by a lead stove placed in the center, and the flames of which pass downward through a large flue in the tank. Fire is kept up for 8—10 hours, but the liquor remains 24 hours in the tank. Pig iron is placed in a bank around the sides of the tank. The temperature reaches about 60° C. Reverberatory furnaces are also used for this work. They have a bottom laid in hydraulic cement, hold 17 cubic meters, and the liquor is heated by the flames passing over it.

Crystallization. After the cementation is complete, the liquor runs to clarifying vats where the fine copper, and the basic salts in suspension in the liquor settle to the bottom. It then marks about 37° B. and is transferred to the crystallization vats, which are wooden tanks, some being 2·20 × 3·00 × 0.50 meters, and others 8·30 × 3·50 × 0·50 in size. Here the liquor remains as long as it is desired to continue the deposition of crystals. Agordo is cold in winter and dry in summer; and as crystallization practically depends partly upon evaporation but mostly upon the depression of the temperature, the place is well fitted for the manufacture of copperas. By leaving the liquor in the vats three or four months, the greater part of the iron sulphate could be obtained. But the production of Agordo is far in excess of the demand, so that there is no neeed to push the extraction so far. Practically the liquor remains 3—6 weeks in the vats. The crystals of sulphate collect on the bottom, on twigs suspended in the liquor, and on the sides of the tank, and these conditions afford three qualities of copperas. That collected on the bottom is the poorest, being contaminated with basic iron sulphate, which is insoluble, but is formed in such a fine condition as to separate completely from the liquor only after long standing. The copperas on the twigs has a certain amount of bark and woody matter in it; that on the sides is pure and of a fine color. If the tanks do not yield enough of this quality to satisfy the demand, the mother liquor, after the first crop of crystals has been obtained, is concentrated in the reverberatory furnaces. It then yields altogether first quality crystals. In the ordinary process of crystallization the strength of the liquor sinks from 37° B. to 26° B.

The composition of this sulphate is as follows:

Ferric sulphate	49·73
Zinc sulphate	4·55
Hydrated Ferric oxide	3·20
Water	42·52
	100

The amount of copperas which Agordo is capable of producing each year is immense. If we assume the percentage of ferric sulphate in the liquor to increase 0·064 per cent. for each degree of BEAUME, we have 0·704 per cent. which can be extracted from the liquor, by lowering its density from 37° to 26° B. That is, we have 774 pounds of ferric sulphate from each cubic meter of cement liquor. RIVOT says that each cubic meter will easily give 600 k. or 1320 pounds. In 1865 Agordo produced 7360 cubic meters of rich liquor and 1967 cubic meters of poor liquor. The rich alone would yield, at RIVOT'S estimate, 4416 tons of copperas. But the production for the year is reported at only 754 tons. Agordo is so far from a market that its profit on this product is very small, and from its impure nature the demand is not great.

The operations connected with mining and the wet treatment, in 1865. dealt with the following quantities of material:

TABLE OF ORE MINED [3].

1. Best ore	containing	7·4 per cent. copper	843	tons containing	62 tons copper.
2. Good	" "	3·1 per cent. copper	5005	" "	155 " "
3. Poor	" "	0·87 per cent. copper	10531	" "	92 " "
4. Small ore.	Good containing	2·48 p. c. copper	711	" "	18 " "
	Poor "	1·25 p. c. "	2261	" "	28 " "
			19,351		355

Average percentage of copper 1·8

TABLE OF ROASTING.

The Roasting piles received bricks and fine ore for covering			4,356 tons.
coarse ore			17,403 tons.
Total			21,759 tons.
Wood consumed, cubic meters			201·61
" " cords			56·7
Labor	Roasting	2869 days	
	Breaking out kernels	39121 days	41990 days.
Per ton of ore:	Wood, cords		0·0029
	Labor, days : roasting	0·132	
	breaking	1·800	1·932
Results:	Kernels	2,324 tons containing copper	145·5 tons.
	Shells	17,667 " " "	209·5 tons.
	Rich ore	475 " " "	33·7 tons.
	Total [4]	20,466 tons.	388·7 tons.

TABLE OF LIXIVIATION.

Shells treated	17,667 tons containing copper	209·5 tons.
Yield : Liquor	12,781 cubic yards containing copper	116·3 tons.
Loss		93·1 tons.

Loss calculated on copper in shells is...44·5 per cent.
Loss " " " " all ores is..23·8 "
Labor 1471 days or 0·07d per ton.

3. This table is computed on 11 months and 9 days only.
4. The difference between this total and that given above is due to piles which were ot fully roasted.

TABLE OF CEMENTATION.

Charge :..... Shells...........17,667 tons containing copper........209·5 tons
Product. . .Rich liquor......10,086 cubic yards.
Poor " ...... 2,695 " "
Cement copper, rich 188·7 tons / " " poor 49·5 " containing copper.....116·3 tons.

Loss.. 93·2 tons.
Loss therefore.. 44.5 p. c.
Fuel :....... Peat........(4·9 per cent. of shells).................... 858 tons.
Charcoal....(= 0·023 per cent. of shells).............. 691 bush.
Iron...320·4 tons.

These amounts give the following as the expense per ton of shells :

Charge :.....Shells............1 ton containing copper..........23·70 pounds.
Rich liquor.......0·57 cubic yards.
Poor " ....0·16 " "
Cement copper...0.135 tons containing copper......13·16 pounds.

Loss........(= 44·5 per cent.) .... 10·54 "
Fuel :....... Peat.........97 pounds (= 4·9 per cent.)
Charcoal ....0·039 bushels.
Iron:..................36·23 pounds.

The expense per ton of pig copper produced is as follows

Charge :.....Shells............1519 tons containing copper.......3602 pounds.
Cement copper.... 2382 pounds " " ......2000 "

Loss........(44·5 per cent.).......................1602 "
Fuel :....... Peat........14,780 pounds.
Charcoal.... 6 bushels.
Iron.................... 5,510 pounds.

THE TREATMENT BY FUSION.

The process consists in fusing the kernels, rich ore and cement copper with sandstone as a flux ; the rich scoria obtained in this and succeeding operations being added for the sake of their copper. The furnace employed is very peculiar, the back and front walls being strongly inclined to the horizon. The furnace is, therefore, in effect, an ordinary shaft, tilted over about 12 degrees from the perpendicular. The object of building it in this way is to make the ore pass slowly through the furnace, the inclination of the back wall increasing the friction ; and also to oblige the gases to follow the front wall and mix with the ore as little as possible in order to avoid too great reducing action. These dispositions have for their object the prevention of iron sows, and the proper preparation of the materials, during their descent, for fusion in the crucible. It is hardly worth while to discuss forms so peculiar, and so little likely at this day, to meet with copyists. But similar constructions have, in times past, been common in Europe, as in the Hartz. They have now been abandoned in most quarters, but it may be well to point out that, with ores rich in iron, sows can be better prevented by a rapid smelting, than by any other means ; and if this rapid fusion does not permit the necessary preparation of the materials in the furnace, they can be prepared before they enter it. This preparation in the furnace consists, according to the Agordc view, partly in driving off the sulphur, and partly in heating the materials. But sulphur can be eliminated to but a very small extent in the shaft furnace. Raw ores, such as the greater part of those smelted at Agordo, practically are, can hardly lose more than 4 per cent. of their sulphur in passing through the furnace, a quantity which could be eliminated by roasting one-twentieth part of the ores before charging. With the Agordo system of building is connected the very serious defect of short campaigns. Eighteen days was the average of the furnaces in 1865. By roasting (if necessary) a part of the ores and smelting 12—15 tons daily instead of 9, and using a straight or a flaring urnace, the campaigns might be trebled in length, and the cost of working reduced.

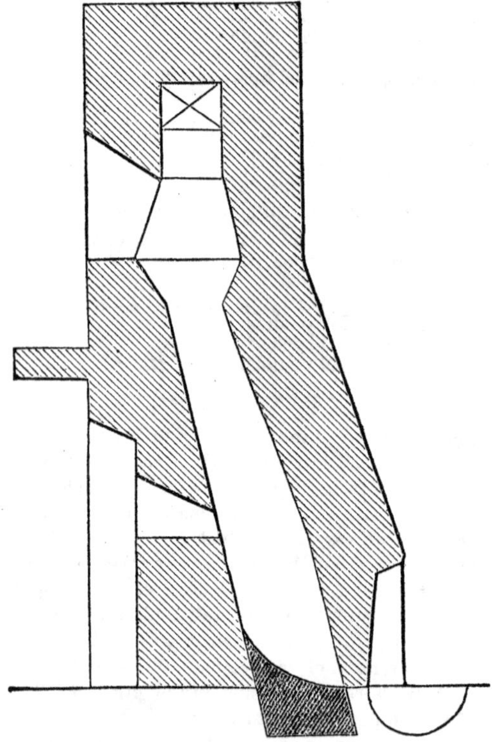

Figure 1.

Figure 1 represents a section, from front to back, of the furnace used for the fusior of ore.

By reference tc the tables further on it will be seen that the expense of fuel per ton of charge is, in the fusion of ore, about 25 bushels per ton, and in that of matte 37 bushels ; the former being 15 and the latter more than 22 per cent. of the charge. This expense would probably be considerably reduced by the adoption of furnaces less wasteful of fuel and capable of maintaining longer campaigns. Even at Lend where the campaigns, for lack of ore, are confined to a week's run, or less, the expense of fuel is no greater.

The resulting matte contains about 24 per cent of copper. It is roasted in piles six times and smelted with sandstone and rich scoria. The furnace is again inclined, but less so than before, as figure 2 shows. It is important, in this operation, to prevent the reduction of too much iron which would make a highly ferriferous black copper. The siliceous flux used at Agordo costs $1.36 a ton, and as it contains about 10 per cent. of iron the amount must be increased over that which would be necessary if the quartz were purer. It is, therefore, an object to smelt with a charge as basic as possible, a treatment which increases the danger of reduced iron.

From this operation black copper of 95 per cent. copper and a richer matte, containing about 60 per cent. copper, are obtained. The former is fined in a common German hearth, and the latter is roasted and returned to the same operation.

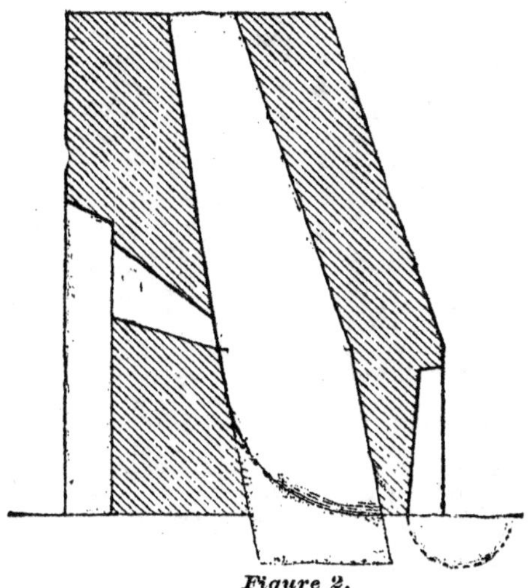

Figure 2.

TABLES OF THE TREATMENT BY FUSION.—FUSION FOR MATTE.

Charge :		Per cent. of copper	Tons
Best ore	containing	7·05	447 tons
Kernels	Best	8·67	251
	Good	6·39	1752
	Poor	3·37	287
Rich cement copper		58·57	188
Poor cement copper		9·89	26
Crasses & Cinders		34·50	106
Scoria			546
Sandstone			579
			4182 tons.

Product :....	Matte containing 23·25 per cent. copper	1285·0 tons.
	Crasses " 10 " "	14·9 "
	Cinders " 15 " "	11·3 "
		1311·2 tons.

Labor :......	16 campaigns, or 843 shifts of 8 hours each ; 4 men to each shift	3372 days.
Fuel :.......	Charcoal 4735 cubic meters	106,310 bushels.
Charge smelted in 24 hours		14·8 tons.
Labor.......	per ton of charge	0·8 days.
Fuel........	" " "	25·4 bushels.
Loss :.......	The charge contained of copper	642,088 pounds.
	The products " "	603,742 "
	Loss therefore " "	38,346 "
	Or	5·9 per cent.

ROASTING OF MATTE.

Matte	1488 tons	per ton.
Charcoal	18288 bushels	12·3 bushels.
Wood	251 cords	0·15 cords.
Peat	55·4 tons	0·03 tons.
Labor	5040 days	3·15 days.

FUSION FOR BLACK COPPER.

Charge :....	Roasted matte containing 23·2 per cent. copper	1343 tons.
	" " " 60.8 " " "	175 "
	Crasses and cinders	25 "
	Scoria	380 "
	Sandstone	477 "
		2400

Products :...	Matte containing 60·26 per cent. copper	191·6 tons.
	Black copper containing 90 " " "	314·4 "
	Crasse 15 " " "	20·3 "
	Cinders 10 " " "	12·8 "
		539·1

Labor :.....	747 shifts, 4 men to each shift	2988 days.
Fuel :.......	Charcoal	88,047 bushels.
Labor :.....	per ton of charge	1·24 days.
Charcoal :...	" " "	37 bushels.
Charge smelted in 24 hours		9·5 tons.
Loss :.......	The charge contained of copper	869,411 pounds.
	The products " "	837,016 "
	Loss therefore	32,395 pounds.
	Or	3·7 per cent.

FINING.

Charge :.....	Black copper	628,443 pounds.
Product :....	Rosette "	492,840 "
	Crasses and cinders	96,228 "
Labor :		1,296 days.
Fuel :.......	Charcoal	24,000 bushels.
Loss :......	Copper in materials charged	597,025 pounds.
	" " obtained	589,068 "
	Loss therefore	7,957 "
	Or	1·33 per cent

TABLE OF LOSS.

	Copper in charge.	Copper in products.	Loss.	Per Cent.
Lixiviation............	418,895 pounds.	232,606 pounds.	186,289	44·5
First fusion...........	641,641 "	603,742 "	37,899	5.9
Second fusion.........	869,400 "	837,016 "	32,384	3·7
Fining..............	597,025 "	589,068 "	7,957	1·33
	2,526,961	2,262,432	264,529	

This amounts to a loss of 34·42 per cent of the copper in the ores. But this is too high, because all the products from the piles and the cementation vats were not smelted within the year. Knowing the percentage of loss on each operation we can calculate the true loss on 20,466 tons of ore containing 388·7 tons copper as follows :

Lixiviation loss on....	418,800 lbs. copper	@ 44·5 per cent.	=	186,366 pounds.
First fusion " "	590,834 " "	@ 5·9 " "	=	34,859 "
Second fusion loss on.	555,975 " "	@ 3·7 " "	=	20,571 "
Fining " "	535,404 " "	@ 1·33 " "	=	7,139 "
Total............	777,400 lbs.	32·0 per cent.		248,935 lbs.

Engineer Pellati reports the loss for 1865 at 31·8 per cent.

From this it appears that roasting and its accompanying lixiviation are the processes which cause the greatest loss, and are, therefore, the least perfect.

Expense per ton. To ascertain the average cost of one ton of pyrites, we will take the following amounts; best ore 406,547 k., kernels 2,081,447, shells 16,060,785 k. ; total 18,548,779 kilos or 20,399 tons. The expenses of labor and material upon each ton of this, in all the operations, is as follows :

TABLE OF EXPENSE FOR 2000 POUNDS ORE, IN UNITS OF LABOR AND MATERIAL.

	Labor days.	Wood Cords.	Char-coal bushels.	Peat tons.	Iron pounds.	Sand stone tons.
Roasting ore..............	1·93	0·003	....	......	....	....
Lixiviation..............	0·07	....	....	......	....	....
Cementation..............	0·12	....	0·034	0·042	31·41	....
Fusion for matte..........	0·17	....	5·160	......	....	0·028
Roasting of matte.........	0.25	0.012	0.900	0·002	....	....
Fusion for Black Copper...	0·15	....	4·310	......	....	0·023
Fining....................	0·06	....	1·18	......	....	....
	2·75	0·015	11,584	0·044	31·41	0·051

Prices at Agordo are as follows :

Mining ore......	9·55	francs per ton	=	$1·91
Charcoal........	12·25	" per cubic meter	=	8·5 cents per bushel.
Wood...........	3·00	" " " "	=	$2·13 per cord.
Peat............	3·00	" " " "	=	$15·00 per ton.
Iron............	150·00	" " 1000 k.	=	$27·26 per ton.
Labor..........	1·00	" " day (average)	=	20 cents a day.
Sandstone.......	7·50	" " 1000 k.	=	$1·36 a ton.

From the above table of loss it is apparent that the old process in use at these works was a very expensive one, considered in regard to extraction. The loss in lixiviation was enormous, and improvement in that part of the process would evidently afford the best reward. But this truth was not immediately perceived ;

a number of minor matters first received attention, and the changes introduced were not always useful.

Improvement at Agordo first took the direction of attempts to increase the amount of sulphur extracted ; and to concentrate the copper more perfectly in the kernel. Although the ore contains 50 per cent., or more, of sulphur, the piles save at most one half per cent. To increase the yield the "Styrian Kiln" was adopted. This is merely a rectangle, enclosed by walls and paved with stone. In the walls, which are very thick, there are a number of chambers, communicating with the interior, by small passages. The ore is filled in and covered with fine ore, and fine spent ore from the lixiviation vats is stamped on the top for a cover. The ore is ignited by a canal in the bottom of the kiln, and the roasting goes on precisely as in a pile ; but the products of combustion are discharged through the side passages. As the sulphur vapors are longer in passing out, and the masonry in which they circulate is exposed to the air, they are more thoroughly cooled and condensed. At the same time the thick walls serve to retain the heat of the mass, which reaches a temparature probably considerably higher than that of the pile. The result of these conditions is, that nearly one-half more sulphur is condensed, and the higher heat produces better kernels. Indeed, poor ore, that gives no kernels, when roasted in piles, yields them in the kilns. The experiment was therefore a success, in having fulfilled the expectations formed of it. But this was the turning point in Agordo improvement. The high heat which made the kernels so fine, also caused the destruction of the copper sulphate, in the shells ; the sulphuric acid was driven off, and copper oxide left. This is insoluble in water, and caused a great increase of the loss in the process of lixiviation, a loss which, as we have already seen, reached 44·5 per cent of the copper treated. The sulphur at Agordo is always contaminated with arsenic, and its use is restricted. Its price is therefore low, and its production unimportant. These considerations led at once to the disuse of the Styrian kiln, (5) and improvement took its true direction in efforts to increase the yield of copper and lessen the expense of operations subsequent to the roasting. Great results have been attained in this work. They are—1st. The almost complete extraction of the copper by roasting and lixiviation ; 2d. Projected improvements in cementation, which include the disuse of all operations but Roasting, Lixiviation, Fining and Crystalization.

Improvements in Roasting—One of the peculiarities of the Agordo deposit is a layer of hygroscopic pyrites, which falls to pieces upon contact with the air. This is made into round, conical bricks, which are dried and then piled like the other ore. But to save the expense of ovens, which are necessary in the winter, the extraction of this ore has been confined to the summer season. It is now proposed to build crushing works, and break up all the ore, except the richest, to the size of one centimeter (0·4 inch). It will then be stamped into bricks. These have the shape of a truncated cone, with a height of 10 centimeters (4 inches), and a mean diameter of 15 centimeters (6 inches.) Three moulds are cast in one

---

5. One of these kilns is still in use, but only for want of room for the roasting piles.

piece, and a workman can make 600 bricks by four o'clock P. M., his work being as follows: bringing and wetting his ore with mother liquor from the crystalization vats; forming the bricks, and carrying them to the drying ground. It should be remarked in regard to the time, that the workmen at Agordo are compelled to leave work at 4 P. M., because of the sulphurous acid vapors from the roasting piles, near which they work. There is nothing in the work itself which forbids a full day's labor, and a production of at least one-sixth more. The bricks weigh about 2 k. or 4·5 pounds each. They are air dried, and then piled on the outside of roasting piles in full operation, and completely dried. The weak solution of iron and zinc sulphates, which forms the spent liquor from the crystalization vats, acts with a slight oxidizing effect upon the grains of pyrites, and binds them together like a cement; the bricks are consequently quite hard.

After drying they are piled in regular order, 70,000 or 80,000 in a pile; covered with small ore, and lighted as usual with logs of wood placed at the corners. When fully ignited a layer of spent roasted ore from the lixiviation vats is thrown over the pile to serve as a cover. The roasting period is, as usual, 7—9 months, according to the size of the pile. This is then opened, and each brick is broken in two to ascertain whether it is fully roasted. Those which are underburned are thrown into a pile of fresh bricks and reroasted. It is the peculiarity of this method that no brick is ever *over*-roasted, a fact that is fully proved by fifteen years' uniform experience.

A perfect roasting, for purposes of lixiviation with water, is that which leaves the greatest possible amount of sulphates. How much superior this roasting of the ore in brick form is over that in lumps, is shown by the following results communicated by Signor de HUBERT:

Fine ore, stamped in moulds, roasts to a red-brown color and loses in lixiviation....	30 @ 32 per cent.
Ore in lumps, well roasted, but of a darker color, loses....	18 @ 25 " "
The same, over-roasted, nearly black in color, loses........	14 " "

Thus we see that the gain by crushing and moulding the ore is twofold. Over-roasting is steadily avoided, and the roasting is better than the best in any other form.

This gain in soluble matter is of course principally iron sulphate, but it is a well-known fact that copper sulphate is much less easily decomposed by heat than iron sulphate, and we ought therefore to expect an increase in the proportionate extraction of copper even greater than that of the iron salt. If we take the average extraction of iron sulphate, from the lump ore, to be 22 per cent., and from the brick ore 31 per cent., the latter gives about 33 per cent. greater yield of this salt than the former. We have seen that the loss of copper in roasting and lixiviation is estimated at no less than 44·5 per cent., while experiments on the new method indicate a loss of only 3 or 5 per cent., which is a gain in extraction of 75 per cent. These results are astonishing, and, simple as the means taken to produce them are, must be underlaid by some general principles of value.

Were the molecules of which each lump of ore is composed independent of each other, we should probably have an almost complete conversion of the sulphide into sulphate in roasting, as the heat produced by the combustion of one extra atom of sulphur does not seem sufficient to destroy the sulphate salt formed by the burning of the other. When this destruction does take place, it is probably due to the fact that the particles of ore do not all reach the sulphate stage at the same moment, and those that arrive there first are subjected not only to the effects of the heat stored up in them by the combustion of their sulphur, but also to the added heat which the neighboring particles of sulphide give out in burning. Among the remedies, which have been proposed for this evil, is the admixture of inert substances to keep the particles of roasting matter apart. The improvement at Agordo may properly be placed in this class, though the substance mixed in with the ore is not a solid, but a gas ; it is air. But the air performs the functions of an inert non-conductor, and it is to this property that it owes its value.

The reason why the bricks roast better than the lumps is doubtless to be found in the difference in the physical condition of the ore, produced by crushing, or by the natural disintegration of the hygroscopic ore. The superiority of the small ore is in the severance of the mathematical contact naturally existing between ore particles, in large lumps. That it plays an important part is proved by the fact, that no kernels are ever found in the bricks formed of small ore, the concentration of copper in the centre being prevented by the separation of the lump into an infinite number of small grains, which have no perfect contact. In the kernel roasting, for which this place has been so famous, it has been observed that the copper in one lump has sometimes been concentrated in a neighboring lump, lower in the pile, with which it came in contact. For the transmission of copper from one lump to another by any process yet suggested, an absolutely mathematical contact is indispensable. Whatever the true method of that transmission may be, it is evident that an action, so exceedingly slow and delicate as it must be, could not proceed if the least chasm or other obstruction lay in the way of the advancing copper. There must have been a mathematical contact between the two lumps of ore, and it remains to explain why two neighboring grains in a brick cannot come into equally intimate union.

The explanation given at Agordo for the transfer of copper from one ore mass to another, is that, in a pile made up of irregular lumps, there will be irregularity of interstices also, and some of the open spaces will be so large as to furnish air enough to cause too rapid combustion in the pieces immediately around them. The heat being thus raised, the mass of pyrites melts superficially, and flows down upon the lump below, thus establishing the close contact necessary for the transmission of the copper, in its process of concentration.

In the brick made up of grains, none of which are larger than 1-16 cubic inch and most are from 1-4 to 1-10 inch in diameter, this rapid fusion cannot proceed. Even if one particle gets into furious combustion, the air which almost surrounds it prevents the transmission of its heat and there is no general fusion of the surface of the brick. Thus the air maintains the disaggregation of the pile.

Admixture of an inert solid, like silica or shale, serves the same purpose as air. The poor ore at Agordo rarely has kernels, or only inferior ones. The interposition of the silica prevents the advance of the copper ; and when kernels are formed it cannot be doubted that the gangue, always small in quantity, is absent, or nearly so, from those pieces which give the kernel. Thus we may refer the slow and even roasting of the bricks to the separation of the ore particles which is accomplished by crushing; while the maintenance of this separation is due to the non-conductor—air—by which they are nearly surrounded.

These facts may be observed daily at Agordo. The piles made up ore bricks are much less aggregated by fusion than the others. Ordinary piles are found to consist, after burning, of a mass which has gained decided coherence by the heat it has undergone. The ore must be knocked out by strong blows of a hammer; while the bricks, though somewhat coherent, yield much more readily.

It is proposed to take advantage of these results of many years experience and erect (1) Crushing works in which whatever crusher is selected will have to exert both a crushing and a percussive action, as the Agordo ore is very hard and tough; (2) Ovens for drying the ore. (The order for these had been received in 1869.) In addition to this, there will probably be some changes in manipulation, as at the lixiviation tanks where the ore is now moved twice, instead of pumping the liquor, a much less laborious operation; but of this kind of improvement which is merely the reforming of a bad disposition of the works, and includes no principle, I do not intend to speak.

The next field in which improvement is to enter is the precipitation of the copper by iron. Three propositions are now before the government, as follows. 1. Hot precipitation in revolving casks, 12 feet in diameter, as at Skofie in Austria. This operation is thus shortened to 12 hours, no basic salts are produced, little arsenical salt precipitated and the amount of iron used is practically a *minimum*; 90 iron to 100 cement copper or 154 iron to 100 pig copper. It is difficult to institute a fair comparison between the Skofie method and that at Agordo, though the ores have about the same value, because the ore of the former is already an oxide; but leaving out the roasting in both cases, the following comparison of loss and expense of material, in other operations, gives a good idea of the decided differences in the two systems.

To produce 1000 k. (2200 pounds) rosette copper, requires at

	Agordo.	Skofie.
Copper in the ore	1412 kilos.	1202 kilos.
Wood	1·90 cubic meters.	
Peat	19·10 " "	
Charcoal	34·40 " "	5·1 m.
Iron	2750·00 kilos.	1540 kilos.
Sandstone	4460·00 "	1540 "

This comparison is the more striking when we remember the fact that only 46 per cent. of the copper which was smelted at Agordo had passed through cementation. The rest was obtained from kernels and rich ores.

2. Addition of sulphuric acid to the liquor during cementation. This is the suggestion of Signor DE HUBERT, director of the smelting works, who has worked out the method. The greatest defect of the present system of precipitation is the production of basic salts of iron. These are the result of the long contact of the hot liquor with the pig iron in the tanks and they cause a loss of iron, a precipitation of arsenical salts, and by adulterating the cement obtained, they prevent the immediate conversion of the cement to pig copper, and thus cause a loss of 9 per cent. of the copper in the cement, by the double fusion which is necessary.

Signor DE HUBERT finds that these inconveniences can be avoided by the addition of sulphuric acid to the cement liquor, a course which carries with it only two objections; the cost of the acid and the use of more iron; while its advantages are the production of a cement which can be smelted at one operation to fine copper; and a larger make of copperas. The latter, it is true, arises partly from the sulphuric acid added and the extra amount of iron consumed; but also, from the prevention of the basic salts.

Experiments in the laboratory gave the following results:

Without sulphuric acid, the cement contained 1—3 per cent. of arsenic and 30 per cent. of copper, the impurity being chiefly basic iron sulphate.

With sulphuric acid the cement contained no arsenic, no basic salt, and 67—73 per cent. of copper; the impurities being carbon from the iron, iron powder, ore particles and sulphur. The latter was in so small quantity that the cement was well adapted for immediate fining.

An experiment in the large way resulted as follows:

Amount of cement liquor (charge for one vat) 16·75 cubic meters.
Concentrated acid 1·25 litres (4 lbs.)
Iron consumed to 100 copper 232·00
Cement contained copper 75·3 per cent.
Arsenic none.

The importance of avoiding the formation of basic salts is seen from the fact at of the cement obtained in 1865:

375,800 pounds contained only	58·57	per cent. copper	=	220,106
51,790 " " "	9·89	" " "	=	5,122
Total copper.............pounds....				225,228

Allowing 33 per cent. for impurities by the proposed method (see experiment in the large way) the production of cement to yield this amount of copper would be 297,007 pounds. As the amount by the old method was 427,590 pounds, we may look upon the difference, or 130,583 pounds, as the amount of the basic salts. These salts have the following composition:

Sulphuric acid............	35 35	
Ferric oxide.............	43·21	Iron 30·24
Alumina.................	15·71	
Zinc oxide...............	5·53	
	96·80	

In addition to this they contain a variable quantity of water.

The enormous consumption of iron, two and three quarter pounds, for every pound of copper precipitated, in 1865, is, therefore, partly due to the formation of these insoluble salts; for they are formed by the union of a certain quantity of the soluble sulphates with the iron introduced into the vat. But the amount of iron thus taken up is only a little less than 22 parts for every 100 of basic salt, or about 29,000 pounds of iron thus wasted in that year. This does not by any means account for the quantity of iron used. But an analysis of the liquor obtained from Agordo ore, shows that it contained an average of one-half per cent.

of sulphuric acid. As there were 345,087 cubic feet of liquor, the amount of free acid was 108,340 pounds. The statement for 1865 would therefore be as follows:

Necessary to precipitate the copper	195,610	pounds iron.
Taken up by basic salts	28,601	"
" " free sulphuric acid	72,226	"
	296,437	
Amount of iron used	640,800	
Amount not accounted for	344,363	

Thus we are unable to trace more than half of the iron which is consumed. If we allow 6 per cent. for carbon and other impurities in the iron, and an equal amount for the iron sand always found in the cement, we should have a further deduction of 41,324 pounds. It may be that ore roasted in the lump contains more free acid than that roasted in bricks, which was used in obtaining the liquor analysed. It is a little remarkable, however, that the formation of iron salts in a liquor which contains one-half per cent. or more of free sulphuric acid can be prevented by the addition of so infinitesimal amount of free acid as 1¼ liters to 16¾ cubic meters; equal to 16,750 liters of liquor.

3. A third improvement suggested is the precipitation of the copper as a sulphide from the cement liquor. To do this, hydrogen sulphide would be made by heating the rich pyrites with sulphuric acid, or passing steam over hot pyrites, the resulting H_2S being dissolved in water contained in a large chamber. The cement liquor would drop into this liquid and the copper be resolved into sulphide which would then be smelted. The objections to this method are the magnitude of the chambers and generators for hydrogen sulphide which would be required to treat about 345,000 cubic feet of cement liquor yearly; the necessity of manipulating the copper sulphide rapidly to prevent its taking fire, and oxidizing to copper oxide which cannot be worked in the furnace without loss, and the difficulty of handling and compressing so large a mass of spongy sulphide. Assuming the yield of 1865 as a basis we have the following estimate of what would be required for this process:

231,000 lbs. copper requires 116,600 lbs. sulphur to make copper sulphide.
116,600 lbs. sulphur requires 220,000 lbs. pyrites to furnish the sulphur.
116,600 lbs. sulphur makes 1,400,000 cubic feet of H_2S gas.
One volume water absorbs 3 volumes H_2S.
Water required, 470,000 cubic feet.
Or 1,513 cubic feet daily for 310 days.

As the amount of cement liquor, in 1869, was only 345,087 cubic feet, the volume of hydrogen sulphide solution would be more than that of the cement liquor. The iron sulphate would no longer crystallize out. Its production would have to be given up or the liquor concentrated again by boiling, which, considering its extreme dilution, would not be profitable. Thus Agordo is considering one proposition to greatly increase its production of copperas and another, which may do away with it altogether.

The circumstances by which the works are surrounded are such that there is no great difference in economy between these two diverse proceedings. The town is situated so far from routes of travel, that the profits on copperas are nearly swallowed up by the freights; so that a very slight improvement in the yield of copper, or in the cost of working it, might determine the sacrifice of the crystallization part of the process. On the other hand the demand for copperas is good; increased make will cheapen processes, and if a great improvement in yield and cost can be obtained by a method which gives more of this article, there will be an advantage in making it. This advantage will be increased by the fact that Signor DE HUBERT's method gives a fine product.

4. The manufacture of cast or wrought iron from the residues of the lixiviation vats, is another suggestion which was under consideration. These residues, as now produced, would give a cast iron containing about 6 per cent. of sulphur, which, with the present process, would do no harm. By the new method of roasting, the percentage of sulphur would be very much less and would indeed be as low as that of iron made from many good brown hematite ores. As the consumption of iron is about 300 tons a year and it could be made at the works for less than $20 a ton, while it now costs $30, the saving would be considerable. With the new system of roasting there is in fact no reason why good iron, which would readily find a market, should not be made. If wrought iron is made, an open fire will be employed and the unhammered bloom used instead of the pig.

In 1869 the recommendations of Signor PELLATI were confined to the manufacture of bricks, and the erection of a blast furnace to make cast iron. The other proposals were under discussion.

The importance of these changes can be seen at a glance, by comparing the cost of the old and new works. In doing this I will assume that the manufacture of bricks requires the same amount of labor as breaking out the kernels. We would have on the one hand the old process comprising the 7 operations already given, on the other, the new process with 4 operations as follows: Roasting, Lixiviation, Fining and Cementation. There would be a saving upon each ton of ore of about half a day's labor, 13 bushels of charcoal and most of the sandstone. This assumes that the efforts to precipitate in such a way as to obtain finable copper are successful.

The importance to this country of a cheap method for the extraction of copper can hardly be over-stated. There is a vast quantity of 2 and 3 per cent. ore in the United States, lying in deposits that are already known, and scattered through all the States. Cheap and excellent processes are already in use, though not generally so. There are no statistics available for making an exact comparison between the cost by them and by the Agordo method. All that can be pointed out now is the differences inherent in these systems. One works with a very great economy of iron, and the other makes sulphuric acid as a by-product. In efficiency and cheapness they are, so far as I know, very nearly on a par.

The advantage of the Italian method is the extremely low cost of the plant. When the contemplated changes have been made, this expense will be confined to the erection of a few rough roasting sheds, lixiviation vats, and a fining furnace, if the amount of ore will warrant it. The outlay for plant which the other systems require, is offset at Agordo by the interest on the cost of mining. This interest, for 9 months, at one per cent. a month would, on ore that cost $2.50 to mine, amount to 23 cents a ton, and on ore that costs $10 to mine, (as it often does in the West) 90 cents a ton. The other expenses by the new method will be about as follows:

EXPENSE PER TON.

	Labor days.	Wood-cords.	Charcoal bushels.	Iron pounds.	Sand pounds.
Making bricks	0·7				
Roasting bricks	0·3	0·003			
Cementation	0·15	0·030		18	
Fining	0·12		2		10
Total	1·27	0·033	2	18	10

To this there would be a small addition for crushing which could be done by a Blake or other coarse crusher.

The copperas which is a by-product of this method, would be valuable only when the mine was so situated as to enjoy cheap and abundant transportation.

It should be noted that this process is applicable to other and more valuable metals than copper. The careful roasting which retains 97 per cent. of the copper in the form of soluble sulphate would be equally effective with nickel and more so with cobalt. These metals or a mixture of them with copper or iron pyrites can be treated by this process and apparently with great success. In fact ores that contain too little of them to be utilizable by ordinary methods, ought to be valuable when brought under this treatment.

THE MERCURY WORKS AT VALALTA.[1]

A FEW miles from Agordo there is a mercury mine, and, connected with it, an establishment for treating the ore which offers some peculiarities well worth considering. This is the mine and works of Valalta. The mercury is obtained from cinnabar found disseminated generally in minute threads and spots through a mass of decomposed porphyry. The rock also contains iron pyrites and gypsum, the latter being usually in contact with the cinnabar when it is concentrated in small veins, as sometimes occurs. Hand specimens of pure cinnabar are found, but they are rare. As at Agordo, this deposit attracts the attention of the metallurgist chiefly on account of its poverty, and the means used to work successfully an ore of so little value

Three sorts of ore[2] are obtained by hand picking as follows :

Good containing	2·5 per cent.	mercury
Poor "	0·25 "	"
Powder "	0·25 "	"

In one year 4,910,000 k. or 5,400 tons of ore were mined, and the mercury obtained was 17,000 k. or 18·7 tons which gives an average yield of 0·346 per cent. The loss as ascertained at the works was 0·10 per cent calculated upon the ton of ore, so that the value of the ore is as follows :

Yield	0·346 per cent.
Loss	0·10 "
Mercury in ore	0·446 "

It has been found that ore containing no more than one-eighth of one per cent. can be worked in this furnace. The methods by which an ore containing only 45-100ths of one per cent. is treated with profit, are as follows :

The works are so situated that the sorted ore is run in cars on a tramway

1. For the information contained in this paper I am indebted to Signor MANZONI, of Agordo, lessee of the works, and to Signor TOMÉ, manager.

2. A full suite of ores and products of the distillation works can be seen at the New York School of Mines.

directly from the mine to the top of the furnace, and this work is charged to mining account. At the furnace it is thrown into a wood box, which is so made that it can be lifted up, and which is placed close to a hopper which forms the mouth of the furnace. In the roof of the latter there is a small pipe, with a cover which has a water joint. By looking through this pipe the workman ascertains the condition of the ore in the furnace, and by thrusting an iron rod through it he ascertains the height of the materials. The normal height of the ore is 3·5 meters or 11 ft. 8 in. When it has sunk to this level a new charge is made, provided the surface is red.

The slide of the hopper is withdrawn and the charge already in it falls upon the hot ore. The slide is then closed, the iron plate which covers the hopper, and which also has a water joint, is raised, and the new charge is dumped in by tilting the box. Charcoal, to the amount of 2 per cent. of the ore, is thrown on top and the cover is replaced. The weight of the charge is 480 to 560 k.—1056—1232 lbs.—and a new charge is made usually every hour and a quarter. The daily work of one furnace (24 hours) is therefore 9,120 k. or 10½ tons.

The furnace is a shaft, and does not differ from the ordinary HÄHNER furnace. The ore rests upon a large grate at the bottom and after each charge the workman pulls down with a hook an equal quantity of spent ore. It falls into an iron wagon, running on a tramway, which is carried under the furnace by means of an arched way.

The peculiarity of this furnace is its condensation. This is by tubes and chambers similar to those employed elsewhere, but the tubes are of wood and the mercurial vapors are drawn through the condensers by suction, an arrangement very important in its results.

1. It produces perfect draft, so that there is never a return of the vapors to the furnace and out at the furnace bottom, as sometimes happens when the draft is natural. With properly proportioned chambers the condensation is therefore also perfect, and the health of the workmen does not suffer from inhaling mercury vapor. In the 12 years during which this apparatus has been in use, there has been no general sickness, though formerly the hospital, usual to these establishments, had to be maintained and was well patronized. But there are now no cases at the works, except (I believe) one or two which are the result of pure carelessness, or else remain over from old times. Another proof of its efficacy is the revival of vegetation in the immediate neighborhood of the furnace. In former times the lessee had a yearly expense of 30,000 francs in making good the damages by the fumes which escaped from his chimney. He is now entirely freed from this tax.

2. It ensures a constant and regular flow of the vapors from the furnace to the discharge pipe, and thus enables the means of condensation to be properly proportioned to the quantity of fumes, and the rapidity of their discharge.

3. It lowers the tension of the products of combustion in the tubes and chambers a little below that of the atmosphere; the column of gases being somewhat retarded at the furnace end by friction of the air against the ore. For this reason when the traps in the tubes are opened there is no discharge of vapors, but, on the contrary, an entrance of air. The workmen are therefore able to collect

the mercury and soot from the tubes without stopping for a moment the run of the furnace. This, together with the following, permits an uninterrupted campaign of two years.

4. By keeping the amount of air admitted within regular limits, it prevents the overheating of the furnace. If this takes place the mercury vapors leave the furnace at so high a heat that the usual means of condensation are insufficient and a loss of metal ensues.

It is to the excellent condensation and the two years run of the furnace, that we must attribute the economical results which permit an ore containing only 9 pounds of mercury to the ton of 2000 pounds, to be worked.

The furnace with its arrangements for charging, condensing and draft is shown in figure 3.

The following are the details of construction :

Furnace :	Height	6·50	meters.
	Diameter	1·20	"
	Inclination of grate, about	50°	
	Number of grate bars	5	
	Width " "	0·05	meters
	Length " "	1·60	"
	Height of gangway under furnace	2·20	"
	Width	1·30	meters.
Hopper :	Height	1·40	"
	Length of mouth	0·90	"
	Width " "	0·30	"
	Length of slide	2.25	"
Charging box :	Length	1·90	meters.
	Height	0·80	"
	Width	0·80	"
Tubes :	Number to 1 furnace	3	
	Length of iron tubes in masonry	1·40	meters.
	" wood tubes, each section	1·70	"
	Number of sections in each tube	8	
	Diameter of tubes, mean	1·00	meters.
	Whole length of each tube as set up	15·40	"
	Thickness of wood	0·05	"
	Inclination	5°	

Condensation chambers : (The dimensions given are nearly correct.)

Number.	Height.	Width.	Length.
1st	5.50	1·20	3·00
2nd	2·40	1·20	3·00
3d	2·65	2·80	3·40
4th	2·70	2·80	3·40
5th	2·80	2·80	3·40
6th	2·80	2·80	3·40
7th	2·30	1·70	3·00

Cubical contents, cubic feet........5,082

Square feet of external surface......2,000

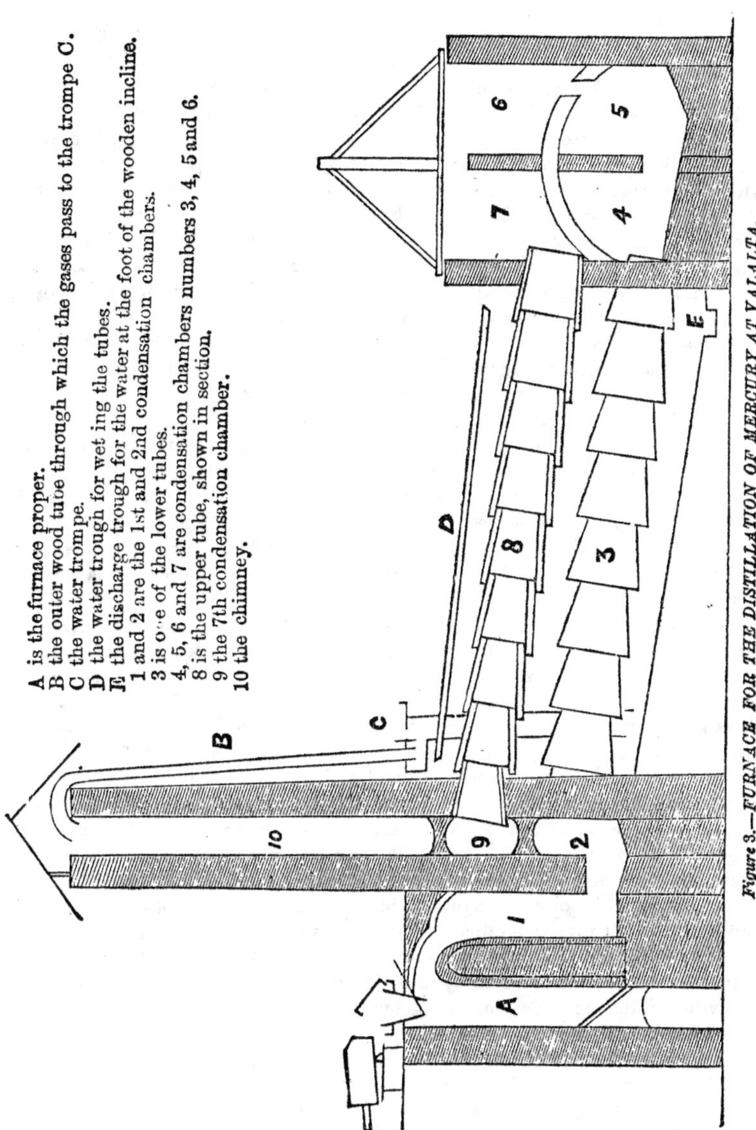

Figure 3.—*FURNACE FOR THE DISTILLATION OF MERCURY AT VALALTA.*

Chimney:.......	Height from arch of 7th chamber	10·00
	Length of wood pipe..........................	10·20
	Diameter " " at top.....................	0·30
	" " " at bottom..................	0·25
	Number of upright wood partitions.............	2

The Furnace is built with thick walls in order to retain the heat. The outer walls are built of slate rock and the lining of large red bricks. Every two years the lining is so worn, from friction of the materials, that repairs are necessary. After the furnace is thoroughly cool, the remains of the old lining are knocked out, from above, and the new bricks are laid with a cement composed of clay, iron filings and acid water from the condensation apparatus. This water contains about 2 per cent. of sulphuric and sulphurous acid. In the outer walls common mortar is used. While making these repairs the workmen are employed only 2 hours a day to avoid sickness from inhaling mercurial dust, as the bricks contain a good deal of the metal. The expense for repairs is, however, slight. After two years, the necessary repairs cost only 150 francs for labor and 50 francs for material; labor being worth about 1—2 francs a day. With very hard bricks which could resist the friction of the ore, there is no reason why the furnace should not have a still longer campaign. The first cost of a double furnace with two shafts, 14 condensation chambers, 6 tubes, and the necessary arrangements for supplying water, is, in Valalta, 20,000 francs. As before said, the furnace with its hopper corresponds in all respects to that invented by Hähner.

The Condensation Chambers. Those nearest the furnace are lined with a cement similar to that used in building the furnace. It is made of ground scoria 2 parts and lime 1 part. The scoria which is much more serviceable than sand, must contain a good deal of iron, as scorias from puddling or reheating furnaces, copper smelting, etc. That used at Valalta is procured in the copper works at Agordo. Those chambers which are placed beyond the tubes are lined with wood 2 inches thick. This is another peculiarity of these works. The wood not only forms a perfectly tight lining when it has been properly seasoned before use, but it affords cleaner mercury and also more of it during the campaign, from the fact that less metal and soot cling to the smooth wooden surfaces than to a cemented wall. Thus, after the first and second chambers, where the vapors are still too hot to permit the use of a wood lining, the fumes have an uninterrupted course through wood or wood-lined passages. After many experiments with cements, bricks, etc., this material has been found the best.

The Tubes are also of wood, 2 inches thick. They are made in sections, slightly conical so as to fit into each other. Wooden wedges, driven firmly into the joints, make the whole tight. Iron tubes were formerly used; but they made a great deal of trouble, being rapidly eaten by the sulphurous acid vapors, emanating from the pyrites in the ore. They had to be turned every 12 or 18 months and entirely renewed in 2 or 3 years. Iron tubes for one furnace cost 8,000 Austrian florins; wood tubes 2,050 florins. But of this sum the 3 iron rings on each section of wood tubing cost 1,200 florins, and as these remain uninjured, the cost of renewing the wood tubing would be only 850 florins, (about $357). But the saving is even greater than this. Though the wood tubes are kept constantly wet, their durability is much greater than that of iron, and I believe they have been renewed only once in 12 years. A main fault of the iron tubes is that the soot obtained from them is contaminated with iron dust and iron oxides, which makes the separation of the mercury from the soot more difficult, and also introduces a certain amount of iron into the metal. All these advantages—cheapness, durability, and serviceableness—give to wood a great superiority when it can be used. Iron tubes are still used for the sections set in the masonry of the furnace and the chambers, but all other sections are wood. It requires a constant and pretty heavy flow of water, and the wood must be of a kind that endures a condition of moisture as long as possible without rotting. Fir and pine are used at Valalta.

Each tube section is bound with 3 iron rings, driven on to the conical tube. Two trap doors are made in each tube, one in the top and one in the side. Through these openings the workman with a long handled hoe, the blade of which is small, draws the soot and mercury on the bottom of the tube to one place and then removes it with a scoop. During this operation his face is protected by a wet sponge placed over the mouth and nostrils. This precaution should never be neglected, though when the trap is opened the appearance of the tube makes it evident that there is little danger of the escape of vapors. The products of combustion are seen as a bluish gray, dense and moist cloud, moving slowly and regularly through the tube, and there is no escape whatever through the open trap; an accident, which if it occurred, could not escape observation, from the strongly marked color of the fumes. But as the workman has his arm at times partially immersed in this cloud, and his face is therefore brought near it, the necessity of using the sponge, as a matter of precaution, is evident. On the bottom of the tube, mercury soot, and metallic mercury lying in small pools are seen, the bright surface of the metal reflecting the light which enters through the trap, and illuminating the tube immediately around it.

The course of the vapors is as follows: from the furnace to condensation chamber No. 1 which has about the same height as the furnace; from No. 1 to No. 2; from No. 2 through the two lower tubes, each 15 meters long, to Nos. 3, 4, 5 and 6 in succession. These four chambers are so connected that all the fluid mercury collects in No. 5, whence it flows through an iron pipe to a kettle placed in a reservoir outside, fed with running water. Both metallic mercury, and mercury white collect in this kettle. Very little soot, and that very poor, collects in the chambers 1 and 2 next the furnace. Most of it falls in the two lower tubes, together with some mercury. A good deal of the latter flows into chambers 3 and 4, and runs into the kettle above mentioned. With so long a campaign it is necessary to collect as much of the metal produced as possible, while the furnace is still in operation; and the arrangements at Valalta for doing this are very perfect. From chamber No. 6 the vapors pass through the upper tube to No. 7, thence to the 1st partition in the chimney, where they rise to the top, return downwards to the second partition, rise again through the 3d partition and finally leave the furnace by a square wood pipe which, turning downwards, rests upon the side of the chimney, and finally at the level of the tubes, or a little above, opens into a water trompe. This has a fall of 5 or 6 meters, discharging its water upon a wooden floor placed under the tubes. This floor, which is carefully made, so as to be water-ana mercury-tight, slopes from the furnace to the condensation house, where the water runs off through a trough, which in its turn empties into a cistern, in order that, by arresting the rapidity of the flow, any mercury that may have found its way to the floor may have an opportunity to settle. There are two ways in which the metal may arrive on the floor : 1st. by leaking through the joints of the tubes ; 2nd. by escaping condensation in its cour e through the various passages until it meets the stream of water. But very little does escape, however, only a few drops ever appearing on the floor or in the cistern. I do not know that any thing of importance has been collected from those places.

The Charge consists of the ore as it comes from the mine, and of bricks made up of fine ore. Much trouble was experienced at first, in making these bricks hard. It was found that to produce a good brick, which would not fall to pieces in the furnace, the ore must not be coarser than one centimeter (0·4 inch) and must be cemented with some substance, like water containing sulphurous acid, or iron sulphate, which by attacking slightly the surfaces of the clay and gypsum in the ore, would act as a cement. The liquor in use is that which serves to condense the last condensable matters in the fumes, and is said to contain 2 per cent. of sulphurous acid. The bricks are made in moulds 10 centimeters (4 inches) high, and with a mean diameter of 15 centimeters (6 inches)· They are dried on iron plates. About one-third of the ore is charged in this form ; but the charge is sometimes one-half coarse ore and one-half bricks.

The Loss in working is, according to the assays continually made at the works, 22·4 per cent. ; or 0·10 per cent. of the ore upon a content of 0·446 per cent. of mercury.

The Products of the distillation are :—1. Mercury. This is very pure and brings the highest price. It is all consumed in Italy and Austria. 2. Mercurial soot. This is composed of mercury in the state of powder, mixed with a little ore powder, mercury sulphide, charcoal powder, etc. It is brought to nature by rubbing it on an inclined table, when the grains of mercury powder coalesce by friction and collect in drops at the bottom of the incline. The remainder is made into bricks and re-distilled. 3. Mercury white, which forms but a very small proportion of the product.

The spent ore, as it is discharged from the furnace is not very hot, gives out no vapors of mercury and only a slight odor of sulphur.

The Labor employed consists of 2 men to each furnace ; length of shift 8 hours ; or 6 men to 24 hours. They bring the charcoal, make the small ore into bricks, charge and discharge the furnace, collect the soot, work it over to extract its mercury, and pack the mercury in sacks of kid skin which are afterwards placed in small kegs. Thus the 6 men complete the *personnel* of one furnace. They are paid at Valalta an average of 1·20 francs (24 cents) a day. Two furnaces require a double number of men.

The Fuel is pine and fir charcoal costing 7 francs a cubic meter ; or 5 cents, coin, a bushel, very nearly ; 600 cubic meters or 18,875 bushels are used for two furnaces yearly.

The Expense of Treatment was given by Signor TOMÉ as follows :

COST OF TREATING 10,000 K. ORE PRODUCING 34·6 K. MERCURY.

	Francs.	Proportions.
Distillation (labor)	15·02	25
Working soot	0·05	0·1
Royalty paid on production	2·30	4·0
Materials	24·78	42
Repairs : labor and materials	1·35	2·4
Running expenses	43·50	73 5
General repairs	3·72	6.3
Administration	11·90	20.2
Cost of distillation	59·12	100·0
Cost of mining	134·73	
Total cost of 34·6 k. mercury	193·85	
Cost of 1000 k. ore, francs	19·39	
Cost of 2000 pounds	$3·53	

The cost is therefor $3·53 for one ton of ore producing 6·92 pounds of mercury, or 51 cents a pound.

The expense for abor and materials upon one ton of ore (1000 k.) is as follows; both labor and materials being included under the head of "repairs."

	Labor.	Charcoal.	Running Repairs.	General Repairs.
For 1000 k.	1·64 d.	84 lbs.	2·7 cents.	7·5 cents.
Proportionate parts. Total cost = 100.	33·5	55·20	3·00	8·30

Mining cost per ton (2000 lbs.)	$2·45	or 69
Distilling	1·08	or 31
	$3·53	100

Though comparisons are never more to be distrusted than when made upon ores of mercury, mined in distant districts and worked in furnaces more or less dissimilar, it is nevertheless instructive to set the results of the Valalta furnace against those in other works. The distinctive characteristics of the HÄHNER furnace is, that it is a shaft and that it works continuously instead of intermittently. Other furnaces are either of the reverberatory form or, if they are built like a shaft, they are intermittent, being filled, fired and cooled down at each operation. Between the HÄHNER furnace at Valalta and those at Idria in Austria and Ripa in Italy, there are two important differences—that of drawing air regularly through the furnace, which is not done at either of the last mentioned places; and the condensation, which is by large chambers and not by tubes, as at Valalta. The work in these furnaces shows some notable differences.

At Idria[3] the ore is charged with 3 to 4 per cent. of charcoal every 1¼ hours.

The ore contains	3·11	per cent. mercury.
The yield is	1·90	" "
Loss therefore	1·21	or 38·9 per cent.

At Ripa[4]

3. Berg. & Hütt. Zeitung, 1854, p. 419.
4. Bull. d. l. Soc. Ind. Min. II., 383.

The charge in 24 hours is 8,800 pounds.
Charcoal 352 " or 4 per cent.
The ore contains 1 per cent.
The yield is only 25—30 per cent.

The system of condensation by chambers is not so thorough as that by tubes, and at Idria and Ripa the condensation is further hindered by the excessive amount of charcoal used, amounting to 50 and 100 per cent. more than at Valalta. This must add very greatly to the temperature of the gases. Whether the regular and moderate flow of air produced by the trompe would effect a reduction of the amount of fuel cannot be told without experiment. The ores are practically the same, except in regard to richness. It should be remarked that poorer ores at Idria require more charcoal.

THE LEAD WORKS AT MECHERNICH.

On the left bank of the Rhine there is a sandstone layer which covers a surface several square miles in area and for a thickness of more than 100 feet, contains lead in the form of sulphide and carbonate. The rock contains but little lead ore, from 2 to 3 per cent. only, but it is so friable as to break up to sand by the mere shock of the blast, and a simple but careful concentration permits the treatment of ore so poor, even, as this. Although this ore does not resemble that which is so common in Utah and Nevada, either in mode of occurrence or in appearance, it has about the same composition. The product consists of about 42 per cent. galena, 28 per cent. lead carbonate, and 30 per cent. quartz and clay. But these proportione are not exact. The amount of silver varies from 0·007 to 0·014 per cent. or 2 to 4 ounces to the ton of washed ore.

The general mode of treatment is by roasting and subsequent fusion with puddle slag and sometimes with metallic iron. There are two works, those of the Mechernich Company and those of Messrs. Pirath & Jung. Three kinds of ore are obtained. Smelting ore, "glasur" ore used for glazing earthenware, and white-lead ore, part of which is worked up to paint by Rhodius Brothers, near Linz, on the Rhine, by means of the gas which issues from natural gas wells.

THE MECHERNICH COMPANY.[1]

Rammelsberg gives the following proportions as the average product of these sorts, at this establishment :[2]

Smelting ore	20,900	tons containing	58	per cent.	lead.
Glazing ore	1,925	" "	62—80	"	"
White lead ore	660	" "	50—52	"	"

ROASTING.

The ore is roasted in furnaces which have a hearth 33 feet long and 12 feet 6

1. For information contained in these notes on Mechernich, I am indebted to Herr Eisenhut, chemist to the company.

2. A full suite of the ores and furnace products of the Mechernich Company are in the cabinets of the New York School of Mines.

inches wide. The roof is made of hollow bricks to lessen the weight and the enormous thrust of an arch so very flat, a weight which soon causes the falling in of an ordinary roof. These bricks are 13½ inches square, 9 inches high, and have a deep depression in their upper surface so that probably two-fifths of the material is removed. The doors are formed of a cast-iron frame set in the brick work, the frame being 2 feet long, 1 foot high and with an opening 8 inches square. This opening is closed by a cast-iron plate.

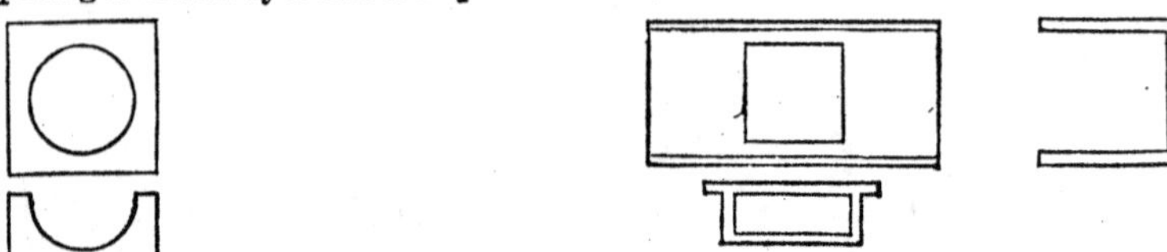

Figure 4. *Figure 5.*

Figure 4 shows the form of the bricks and figure 5 that of the iron castings for the doors.

A cast-iron box on the top of the furnace receives the ore while it is drying. About ninety centners or 9,900 pounds are charged every 12 hours, so that the furnace roasts 9 to 10 tons daily. The rapidity of the roasting depends somewhat upon the proportion of carbonate in the charge. When there is much of this, the roasting is rapid; and the large amount passed through these furnaces is also due to this ore. At Freiberg, where the ore is altogether sulphide, the furnaces cannot work so much. The Mechernich works have 10 of these furnaces.

The management of these furnaces is peculiar. The ore lies in a much thicker layer than is usually allowed, and toward the fire-place it is heaped up nearly to the roof, in the center sloping away to the sides, where the gases mostly pass. Next the fire-place there is a depression in the hearth, called the crucible, designed to receive the ore which is completely melted toward the end of the operation. The ore forms a broad bank at the edge of this crucible, and in immediate contact with the flames. It smelts rapidly, and as fast as the melted ore runs down into the crucible the ore behind it is pushed forward.

But it is evident that this method of treatment is not favorable to the liberation of the sulphur, a process which demands the most complete access of air, and access is prevented in these furnaces by the extreme thickness of the ore layer. Accordingly we find that although the ore cannot contain more than 5 per cent. sulphur, as a great part of it is already oxidized and there is no pyrites present, the roasting is still far from perfect. When the ore arrives at the crucible it does so with its galena probably not more than half roasted and the melting down of the fine and intimately mixed quartz and lead oxides is then so rapid that the galena is covered with a glaze of slagged ore. It is carried down with the latter into the crucible and forms a layer under it. I should judge the furnaces were producing, at the time of my visit, fully 20 per cent. of this unaltered galena.

This artificial galena is very much richer in silver than the ore which has been converted into silicate; a circumstance which is due to the stronger chemism between silver and sulphur than between silver and oxygen. An assay was made at my suggestion of the oxidized ore and the unaltered galena from a furnace, which unfortunately for the trial. was running on very poor ore, containing about 25 per cent. lead.

I. The unaltered galena contained 0·055 per cent. silver or 7·3 ounces per ton.
II. The lead silicate " 0·008 " " " 2·3 " "

To prevent the formation of this product a new furnace has been built. It has two hearths, an under and an upper, with 75 feet of hearth length. This is a success in so far as its roasting is better, its product being an almost completely homogeneous silicate, with but few particles of galena distributed through it. In repeating this experiment a furnace has been built with a total length of hearth amounting to nearly 82 feet. The result has not been made public. There is, however, one difficulty connected with the reduction of the sulphur to so small an amount. Under the old circumstances a certain quantity of matte, about 2 per cent of the charge, was formed and collected at the bottom of the conical pots used to receive the slag. But a less quantity than this would probably elude collection and have to be thrown on the waste heap with the slag. A certain amount of matte is always retained by the slag, either in solution or in minute drops mechanically held. If the sulphur can be reduced to the amount which the slag has always retained in this manner, there would certainly be a gain ; but if the liberation of the sulphur is not carried so far, but still far enough to make the collection of the matte impracticable, there would be a loss.

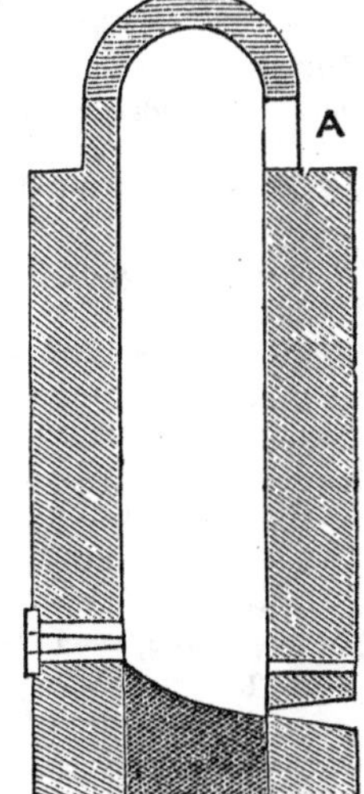

Figure 6. Lead Furnace at Mechernich.
A—Charging Door.

In roasting by the former method it was impossible to ascertain the progress of the operation, for the mass of ore in the furnace was by no means homogeneous. The amount of galena which passed unchanged through the operation proved that it was very incomplete. In the new furnace, however, the amount of sulphur liberated can be ascertained ; and with ore containing 6·5 to 7·5 per cent. sulphur. corresponding to 48·5 and 56 per cent. galena, the roasted ore has 1·5 to 1 per cent., corresponding to 11·2 and 7·5 per cent. galena. The larger of these quantities, 1·5 per cent. sulphur, corresponds to an amount of matte equal to about 6 per cent. of the ore ; but this would be very much lessened by the sulphur dissolved in the slag. Assuming that only one-half the sulphur was formerly eliminated in roasting, we find that about 3·5 per cent. of sulphur in the shaft furnace gave about 2 per cent. of the matte. Reduced to 1·5 per cent. the sulphur would probably all be absorbed by the slags. and the new method would therefore be advantageous. It is hoped, however, that the ore can be entirely freed from sulphur, or the latter reduced to less than one per cent. at most, and in that case there would be a considerable saving by the better roasting.

FUSION.

The Furnaces in which the roasted ore is smelted, are shown in figure 6. They are built of ordinary red brick. They are 15 feet high, and 4 feet square, and have 4 water tuyeres, which are of the built up kind, the back piece being bolted, instead of cast, on. These tuyeres have been discarded in most works. The furnaces are closed at the top by a brick flue, the gases being led to high chimnies which complete the system. Other dimensions are as follows:

Height of furnace	15 feet.
Section, square	4 × 4 "
Height of slag hole above tap hole	14 inches
" " side tuyeres above slag hole	10 "
" " back tuyeres above side tuyeres	6 "
" " " " tap hole	30 "
Length of tuyer	30 "
Diameter of tuyer outside	14 "
" " interior	1¾ "
Material of furnace	Red brick.
Material of hearth, brasque made of	Coal ashes. Clay. Coke dust.

A round furnace had just been finished at the time of my visit, designed according to the principles which gave such success to the Freiberg furnaces. Its dimensions were as follows:

Height	15 feet.
Diameter at top	6 "
" of hearth	4 "

Air is supplied at a pressure of 9 inches of water by two fans made after especial designs. They have the usual tapering vanes and do extremely good service. Their dimensions are.

Diameter	5 feet 6 inches.
Width of blades at center of fan	10 "
" " " circumference	6 "
Diameter of conducting pipe	10 "
Revolutions per minute, maximum	1200 "
" " " when regularly working	800 "

Only one fan is in constant use, the other being kept in reserve. In the blast house the pressure is 10½ to 11 inches of water, which diminishes to 9 at the furnaces. At the time of my visit this fan supplied 5 shafts and 1 cupel furnace.

The Charge. It has been found that a slag which is to be free from lead must contain at least 40 per cent. of oxide of iron, and as the Mechernich ore contains none of this metal, its only impurity being a very small amount of copper, iron has to be added to the charge in some form. For this purpose puddle slag is brought from Eschweiler near Belgium, and when there is any raw ore, or much unoxidized galena in the charge, a small quantity of cast-iron is also added.

The charge is made up as follows:

Roasted ore........56—58 per cent. lead	100	
Puddle slag	50	
Limestone	48	
Iron	2–5	203
Coke = 9·9 p. c. of charge or 20 p. c. of ore		20

At the time when the charge above given was taken down, the works were compelled, for lack of sufficient number of laborers at the roasting furnaces, to add raw ore, which accounts for the iron in the charge. It will be observed that the amount of coke used is very small, a consequence of the fusibility of roasted lead ore. About 35 tons of charge are smelted in 24 hours.

Products. From this operation are obtained :

Lead containing 0·014—0·027 per cent. silver or 4—8 ounces to the ton.
Matte containing 10 per cent. lead.
Slag containing 0·75—1 per cent. lead.

The slag is received in iron pots 2 feet high, 16 inches in diameter at the top and 6 inches at the lower end. In these the matte settles to the bottom, nearly every block yielding 10—25 pounds. But to make this settling of the matte sure, it is indispensable that the pot be rapidly filled. When this system of drawing-off slag was first introduced, several trials were deemed unfavorable which failed only because the slag was allowed to drop slowly into the pot, and the lower half of the contents became solid before the upper half ran in. Perfect fluidity of the mass is necessary for the settling of the matte, and for this reason the furnace must be a closed one ; a form which has many advantages besides the collection of small quantities of matte which might otherwise be lost.

DESILVERIZATION OF THE LEAD.

In former times three out of the five systems of desilverization by zinc were practiced at Mechernich and in its neighborhood. The differences, as with all these methods, were in the method of dezincing the lead after the silver had been removed. These three methods will be considered in describing this and the following works.

At Mechernich the kettles hold 11 to 12 tons each. The zinc amounts to one and one-twelfth per cent. of the lead and is added in 3 portions : (1) 0·75 per cent.; (2) 0 25 per cent. , (3) 0 083 per cent. On 11 tons this is 165 55 and 18¼ pounds ; total 238¼ pounds. The zinc alloy is ladled into moulds and the pigs are heated in a tube slightly inclined. By raising the temperature gradually a good deal of the lead runs out, leaving an alloy much richer in silver. Toward the end of the operation the alloy is stirred with a rod until it becomes quite "dry," and has the form of lumps or shot. It is then melted and cast. Its silver now amounts to 1·5 to 2·5 per cent., but much richer alloy is sometimes obtained.

The lead which runs from this tube contains 0·012—0·020 per cent. silver and passes again through the process of desilverization.

Treatment of the rich alloy. These works long retained the old method, rejected everywhere else, of fusing the rich alloy with puddle slag to remove the zinc. The fusion of silver at a high temperature in the presence of zinc should, according to all laws of metallurgy, be an operation attended with considerable loss, and great care was taken to make this as small as possible.

The furnace was 10 feet high and 2½ feet square, and had 3 tuyeres. It was first started with puddle slag alone, and when this was flowing freely, the alloy was charged.

To 100 of alloy 90 parts of puddle slag were added and smelted with 17—18 coke. The pressure of the blast must not be more than 6 inches of water.

About 7,700 pounds of this mixture were smelted in 24 hours, and the loss is said to have been not more than 1 per cent. of lead at the outside.

The poor lead is de-zinced in a similar manner. It is charged with puddle slag in the proportion of 100 lead, 4 to 5 puddle slag, and 3 to 4 coke. It is then poled and cast. It is very pure, as the following analysis by Mr. EISENHUT, chemist to the Company, shows :

Silver	0·00025
Copper	0·0025
Antimony	0·0050
Iron	0·0030
Zinc	trace.
Nickel	0·0021
Lead by difference	99·98715
	100

THE NEW PROCESS.

Within three years the method of de-zincing by steam has been introduced at Mechernich. When the third alloy has been taken off, steam is introduced for two hours, the lead being kept at a red heat, and covered with a close hood. Then the hood is opened to allow the air to enter and the passage of steam is continued one hour, to remove the antimony. The new method produces more scraps but saves in labor. Its chief advantages, however, are the more perfect removal of antimony and the complete removal of the nickel, which by the analysis last given is seen to be present in small quantity. What alteration the change has had upon the quality of the lead is to be seen from the following average of two analyses, made by Mr. EISENHUT upon lead produced by the steam process :

Silver	0·00052
Copper	0·00175
Antimony	0·00405
Iron	0·00064
Lead by difference	99·99304
	100

The rich lead, now freed of its zinc, is poled for one hour in a kettle, and cupelled in an English furnace, having the ordinary elliptical test, with axes of 3 and 4 feet. The run lasts 5 to 6 days, 13,000 pounds weight of lead is cupelled, and the button of silver weighs about 150 pounds. The tuyere is a pipe 2 inches high and 6 inches wide, the blast passing through a zinc pipe 3—4 inches in diameter. It is the experience of many works, that a large tuyere of this kind makes poorer litharge than one with a narrower orifice.

Treatment of the Matte. Matte amounting to about 2 per cent. of the ore's weight is obtained from the fusion of the ore. It is roasted and smelted with lead scraps to second quality lead. This contains more antimony than the first lead, but still considerably less than one per cent. though sufficient to give it a silvery whiteness. It is partly made up into shot, an old shaft in the mine serving for a shot tower, and the shot being made on English and American account.

THE COMMERN WORKS.

MESSRS. PIRATH & JUNG have a similar establishment in Commern near Mechernich, and treat ore from the same sandstone layer. Their mine, however, produces less galena in proportion to the lead carbonate than the other, and they consequently have less unaltered galena in the roasted ore. The record of two of their roasting furnaces for three weeks is interesting:

	Furnace No. I.		Furnace No. II.	
	Coal lbs.	Ore lbs.	Coal lbs.	Ore lbs.
August 7	28,400	180,500	32,200	186,500
" 14	30 400	176,000	31,800	188,750
" 21	29,400	190,000	30,200	203,000
	88 200	546 500	94,200	578,250

Total ore roasted........................1,124,750 lbs.
" coal consumed.................. 182,400 "

This amounts to a consumption of 16·21 per cent. of coal, and a daily product of 53,580 pounds from two furnaces. There are no analyses of the roasted ore at hand but its composition is pretty nearly: silica 35, lead oxide 55, clay, iron, sulphur, copper and antimony, 10. Limestone is sometimes added in roasting; but only where there is too little lead present.

The furnaces have the following dimensions:

Height	14 feet
Section	4×4
Tuyeres	4
" height above tap	17 inches

The material is red brick and the campaign usually last 3 to 4 months. The charge is composed of

Roasted ore	44,000 pounds.
Unroasted ore	9,900 "
Limestone	18,900 "
Puddle slag	27,500 "
Coke 11—12 per cent.	11,660—12,650 "

The amount reported to be passed through these furnaces daily is enormous; amounting to 132,000—143,000 pounds, and if the Mechernich works, with the same ore and the same furnaces smelt only 38½ tons in 24 hours with 10 per cent. of coke, it is hardly possible that the Commern works put through 66 to 71 tons with 11 to 12 per cent. of fuel. The latter quantities are fully equal to the largest charges the much larger furnaces of Freiberg have run through, when the charge consisted almost entirely of fusible slag.

Each furnace at Commern produces 27,500—28,600 pounds of lead daily. The slag is reported to contain 0·3—0·4 per cent. lead, and the lead about 6 ounces to the ton.

In the method of desilverization (before the introduction of the steam process) there were some differences from that pursued at Mechernich. After melting in the kettle the lead was first poled to remove all impurities. Poling consists in plunging a stick of green wood in the melted metal, which is hot enough to char it rapidly. It gives out a great quantity of gas, partly composed of steam from the large amount of water contained in green wood and partly carburetted compounds resulting from the decomposition of the fibre. The escape of these gases throws the bath into violent ebullition and every part of the metal is brought to the surface, where the lighter alloys of iron and copper with zinc remain. As at the neighboring works 1·08 per cent. of zinc is added in three operations, but the amounts are varied, being 1st. 0·66 per cent., 2nd. 0·34 per cent., 3d. 0·083 per cent.

The chief point of difference is in the treatment of the poor lead, in order to free it from zinc, the old method, suggested when the zinc process was first invented, being in use. The lead is melted in a reverberatory furnace under a layer of coal, on which is a layer composed of salt 2 parts, sand 1 part and lime 1 part. The furnace holds 22,000 pounds lead, which it is treated for 8 to 9 hours and the product is "best selected" lead, the purity of which is sufficiently proved by the following analysis made at Clausthal in 1869 :

Silver	0·0023
Copper	0·0034
Antimony	0·0081
Iron	0·0013
Lead by difference	99·9849
	100

THE WORKS AT CALL.

The works at Call[3] were established for the purpose of working over old slag, left by the Romans, or some less ancient people, and this material is still treated, but the bulk of the the lead is made from purchased ores. The latter are obtained in Westphalia and also at Stolberg. They are mixed with brown spar, copper pyrites, and zinc blende ; the lead contains about one-half per cent. of antimony. Of silver the lead contains about 0·025 per cent. or 7·3 ounces per ton.

As at Mechernich the ore is first roasted ; the furnace being 45 feet long and 7 feet wide with double sole, which gives 90 feet of hearth length. This furnace will hold about 88,000 pounds of ore, which is charged every 6 hours in posts of 3,300 pounds. Four posts are drawn daily so that 13,200 pounds or 6½ tons are roasted daily. Like the Mechernich furnaces there is a deep hearth next the fire place where the roasted ore is melted, and the furnace is tapped every 12 hours. From these figures it will be seen that the ore remains from 6 to 7 days in the furnace.

The blast furnaces at Call are remarkable in these days for having but one tuyere. They are 19 feet high, 4 feet from front to back and 3 feet wide. The top is closed by a hopper built of brick and lined with cement. This hopper is large enough to contain one charge. It is closed by a slide which, being pulled out, lets down the charge. The hearth is narrowed a little to prevent the formation of sows. About 16½ tons of charge are smelted in 24 hours. The blast is by fans and the pressure 8 inches of water. Another furnace is square and has 3 tuyeres.

---

3. Preuss Zeitschrift, 1868, p. 268.

SEPARATION OF SILVER.

The lead which on an average contains 250 grammes silver in 1000 kilograms, or a little more than 7 ounces to the ton, is melted in kettles of 7 feet diameter and 22 inches depth, holding about 25,000 pounds. The dross is taken off, the lead heated until zinc melts readily on it, when 198 pounds of zinc is added, stirred for half an hour and the whole suffered to cool until the zinc solidifies on the surface, when it is taken off. This zinc crust is at first about 3 lines thick but the removal of the surface lead is continued until the lead begins to crystallize which, it has been found, takes place when about 2 inches of the bath have been removed.

The first charge of zinc having been taken off the kettle is filled up with liquated lead, (see below) 68·2 pounds of zinc are added, and after a repetition of the above process a third charge of 38·5 lbs. is put in. By these three charges 304·7 pounds of zinc have been added or close on 1¼ per cent., and the silver left in the kettle is reduced to 0·00055 per cent. or 0·16 of an ounce. The source from which this liquated lead is obtained will be seen below.

The lead originally contained about 0·15 per cent. of antimony and 0·2 per cent. of copper. It now has nearly all the antimony concentrated in the remaining lead, but is nearly free from copper, which has followed the silver in uniting with the zinc.

To remove the zinc a method was formerly employed which was the invention of Mr. Herbst, one of the proprietors of the works. It is to this gentleman that metallurgists owe the re-introduction of the zinc process after it had lain many years neglected. His improvements and perseverance established the process on a successful basis for the first time, and the remarkable advances made in this method during the last ten years had the following process for a starting point, though it has since been abandoned in nearly every works.

The lead containing zinc was heated to a dark red and covered with an intimate mixture of 110 pounds salt and 320 pounds lead sulphate. For lead containing 0·6 per cent. of zinc, about 330 pounds of this mixture was charged to each kettle. Soda sulphate and zinc chloride were formed, but the larger part of the zinc must have been removed as zinc oxide. For 24·750 lbs. lead at 0·6 p. c. contain 1485 pounds of zinc, requiring 163 pounds of chlorine to make ZnCl. But the 110 pounds of salt charged contain only 77 pounds of chlorine, very much of which remains as sodium chloride. The "salt slag" remaining consisted of unaltered sodium chloride, lead sulphate, mingled with zinc oxychloride, soda sulphate and metallic lead. After twenty-four hours the zinc was all removed.

The lead now contained no impurity but antimony, and it was with a view to the removal of this troublesome ingredient that the peculiar kettles used at Call (and I believe no where else) were designed.

Antimony cannot be removed by steam, but requires for its oxidation the slow action of air upon the heated lead. When steam is used for the removal of this metal, as at Mechernich and many other works, it acts merely as a mechanical stirrer of the lead, throwing it up and changing its surface constantly, so that every particle is brought in contact with the air.

At Call after poling the lead for half an hour it is kept a long time, usually 48, sometimes 72 hours at a red heat, and covered by a layer of lime which prevents the volatilization of the lead, but does not hinder the access of the air. Lead containing up to one per cent. of antimony can be softened in this way; that at Call sometimes reaches one-half per cent.

The complete removal of the antimony is ascertained by casting a small ladleful of the lead in a scorifier or assaying crucible. So long as this contracts in cooling leaving a crystalline star in the centre, antimony is indicated. But when there is merely a depression in the centre of the button, with no star, the process is known to be finished.

From these operations results a metal of great purity as the following analysis shows:

Silver	0·0005
Copper	0·0004
Antimony	0 0008
Iron	0·0019
Bismuth	0 0023
Thalium	0·0003
Lead	99·9938
	100

REMOVAL OF ZINC BY ACID.

The management of the zinc alloy is peculiar. The alloy produced by the second and third charges of zinc is kept separate from that obtained from the first addition of zinc. The former is very much adulterated with lead. It is melted in a kettle, the alloy rising to the top, while a "liquated lead" containing about 3·5 ounces silver to the ton remains under it. The temperature is raised nearly to bright red, at which the overlying layer of alloy oxidizes. When this oxidation is complete, the lead is drawn off by a spout, leaving the oxides with nearly all the silver behind. The lead goes back to the second and third additions of zinc as before said.

The oxides are mixed with about one-half tveir weight of chlorhydric acid, at first in the cold and afterwards the solution is completed at a low heat. When this operation is finished the liquid is evaporated until it becomes thick, a sign that all the water is removed. Then the alloy resulting from the first charge of zinc is added. In this the lead and zinc are still in the metallic state and a reaction sets in; the zinc is all converted into chloride and the lead and silver mostly to metal. This process takes 24 hours.

By this means a rich lead containing 1·5 to 2 per cent. of silver is obtained which is cupelled. The method has the advantage of superseding the dezincing of the alloy by steam, an operation not free from hazard, and one that is always a disturbing element in the zinc process.

The residue contains from 20 to 55 per cent. of lead chloride, the remainder being zinc chloride with 17—25 ounces to the ton. We have seen that the zinc in the 2nd and 3d alloys was transformed into zinc chloride by treatment with lead sulphate and sodium chloride at a high heat; the result was soda sulphate and zinc chloride. Precisely the opposite reaction is now produced by mixing these residues containing lead chloride, with "salt slag" obtained in de-zincing the poor lead, and treating them with water acidified with chlorhydric acid.

This acid changes the zinc oxychloride to neutral zinc chloride, which is soluble. Copper chloride and silver chloride are also dissolved, the latter in consequence of the other chlorides in solution. But the lead chloride is transformed to insoluble lead sulphate by reaction with the soda sulphate. We have then the original mixture of salt and lead sulphate restored. After settling, the liquor is run to a vat containing copper where the silver is deposited, and to another containing iron where the copper falls down.

By these separations the liquor now contains nothing but zinc chloride, and iron sub-chloride. The addition of chlorine transforms the latter to per-chloride, which is precipitated by lime. The remaining solution of zinc chloride is heated and the zinc precipitated as oxide by pure lime, super-saturation being carefully avoided. The zinc oxide is finally distilled to metallic zinc.

This process is an excellent example of a simple method of treating the rich alloy by acids, a treatment which in many places is forbidden by the high price of chlorhydric acid. It does not appear that the acid is particularly cheap at Call, but the small percentage of silver in the lead, and the consequently small amount of alloy to be treated, gives the acid method advantages over the treatment by fusion with slag, or by steam. The silver is obtained more quickly than would be the case if the rich alloy had to be accumulated until enough was at hand to fill a kettle, say 15,000—20,000 pounds ; or to support a campaign in the furnace, which would require even more. Thirty centners or 6,600 pounds suffices for the treatment with acid. It is to be remarked, too, that the shallow and extremely wide kettles, in use at this place, may not be well adapted to the use of steam ; though that question is still unanswered, as I believe steam has not been applied to kettles like them. Those recommended by CORDURIÉ are very deep and of small diameter ; while those in the Hartz are 2 feet 10½ inches deep and 5 feet 6½ inches in diameter, and this is about the size of the old Pattinson kettles in most works, which have been used without alteration for the zinc process.

But the process described above is no longer in use at Call. Mr. HERBST has invented another which he keeps secret, unwilling to give his discovery gratuitous circulation and dissatisfied with the Prussian patent laws, which he thinks have not given him protection enough. His new method is said to be cheaper than any other yet introduced.

GOLD AND SILVER WORKS AT LEND.

THE (1) treatment of ores containing gold and silver, by fusion with lead is one of the common operations of metallurgists. A very small establishment of this kind, but in many respects characteristic of the general European practice is found at Lend, in Austria. This place lies in the Salzburg Alps, and receives its ore from the mines at Rauris and Boeckstein. The former lying 8200 feet above the sea is said to be the highest mine in Europe, some of its openings being made in glacier ice.

The ore differs in no way but extreme poverty from countless mines in the West. It consists of gneiss, quartz, chlorite and clay slate ; containing iron pyrites, copper pyrites, arsenical pyrites, galena, blende, and stilbite or sulphuret of antimony. The gold is found in two states : free gold and gold alloyed with silver. This alloy, in 1866 was composed on the average, of 15·33 gold and 84·67 silver, which gives a specific gravity of 11·28. Mercury has a specific gravity of 13·6, and as the amalgamation of gold by the Austrian method, is looked upon as a proceeding entirely mechanical, the separation being effected solely by the superior gravity of the gold over mercury ; this alloy which is lighter than mercury cannot be amalgamated (2). Such is the lesson of long practice, the free or fine gold being extracted from a part of the ore, at least, by amalgamation while the tailings are smelted to obtain the alloy. The following table will show the proportion of fine to alloyed gold and also exhibit the extreme poverty of the ore. To the Rauris and Boeckstein ores are added those from Zell in the same part of the Alps. The ore from the last named place is not now worked, the point of poverty having apparently been reached at which the auriferous rock ceases to be an *ore.*

	Rauris In 2000 lbs. Troy ounces.	Boeckstein In 2000 lbs. Troy ounces.	Zell In 2000 lbs. Troy ounces.
Fine Gold	0·32—0·48	0·098—0·113	0·090—0·097
Auriferous Silver	14·0—14·0	5·700—6·600	unimportant.
Iron pyrites, copper pyrites, galena	8 per cent.	4½ per cent.	unimportant.
Value of Silver and Gold in American coin	$13.49—$16.92	$5.91—$8.49	$1.86—$2.00

As in 1866 Boeckstein delivered 63 per cent. of the ore smelted at the works and Rauris 37 per cent. ; the average value for that year was $10·28 or 0·0009

1. This paper is mainly reprinted from one read before the Institute of Mining Engineers May 22, 1872. For the information contained in it, I am indebted to Dr. LEO TURNER, former director of the works, now at Brixlegg in the Tyrol.

2. See Rittinger, "Aufbereitung" page 469 ; Ed. 1867.

per cent. gold and 0·017 silver. This does not include the value of the copper and lead which form respectively 2 per cent. and 1 per cent. of the ore. The former is extracted, the latter is not sufficient to supply the waste of the process and lead has to be bought for the works. Even in Europe these ores are considered extremely poor. I am not aware that ores from veins as poor as these have ever been utilized in this country, but if they have they owe their value to the fact that the gold is all fine and can be amalgamated.

TREATMENT OF THE ORE.

The ore is first sorted to six varieties for the furnace and one for amalgamation. The former are quartzose ore, rich, medium and poor, compact pyrites, galena and antimonial ores (1).

The quartzose ore consists mostly of quartz with which are gneiss and chlorite it contains iron pyrites, arsenical pyrites, blende, copper pyrites, and a very little galena. Its value in gold and silver is 400—2240 grammes to the ton, or 12 to 70 oz. Of this alloy from 10 to 30 per cent. is gold. This ore gives 20-25 per cent. of raw matte.

Compact pyrites is composed of iron oxide, arsenical pyrites, and copper pyrites, and these are often accompanied by magnetite, when it is usually richer. It is nearly free from gangue. Its content varies between 80 and 400 grammes of gold and silver to the ton; or 2·5—12 ounces. The gold forms about 25 per cent. of the alloy

Glaserz, is a name given to a mixture of quartz and gneiss with disseminated pyrargyrite; silver and antimony sulphide; antimony glance and galena. Its content varies very much, usually between 800 and 2000 grammes, or 26—60 ounces, to the ton, of which 25 per cent. is gold. Most of this comes from Boeckstein.

Glance ore, or fine leaved galena, with 4000 or 5000 grammes, or 140—160 ounces of silver, almost without gold, to the ton.

The *Glaserz* occurs oftenest in quartz; copper pyrites and occasionally peacock ore, in chlorite gneiss; blende, iron pyrites and arsenical pyrites in quartz and gneiss.

The mill slimes are of three qualities, ; 1 and 2 are nearly pure pyrites, having been concentrated in milling, and giving 50—60 per cent of matte. One contains 500—1500 grammes of alloy, of which 7—14 per cent. is gold; two contains 22—75 grammes alloy of which 2·5—4 per cent. is gold; three is the poorest slime from the shaking table. It gives 25—30 per cent. of matte, and contains 300—1000 grammes or 10—40 ounces of alloy, of which 9—18 per cent. is gold. It is used as a siliceous flux. Only the poorest ore containing merely traces of pyrites is sent to amalgamation; which is done because it there undergoes concentration.

The ore for amalgamation is stamped under stamps of 220 pounds weight (total) through sieves of 1.6 mm. (0·06 inch), the stamp chest having a sieve on each

1 A full suite of these ores with the furnace products at Lend can be seen at the School of Mines in New York.

side to secure the most rapid discharge of the slime possible. Two methods of treatment are employed for the slimes :—1. They are first concentrated and then amalgamated ; or, 2. They are first amalgamated and then concentrated. With

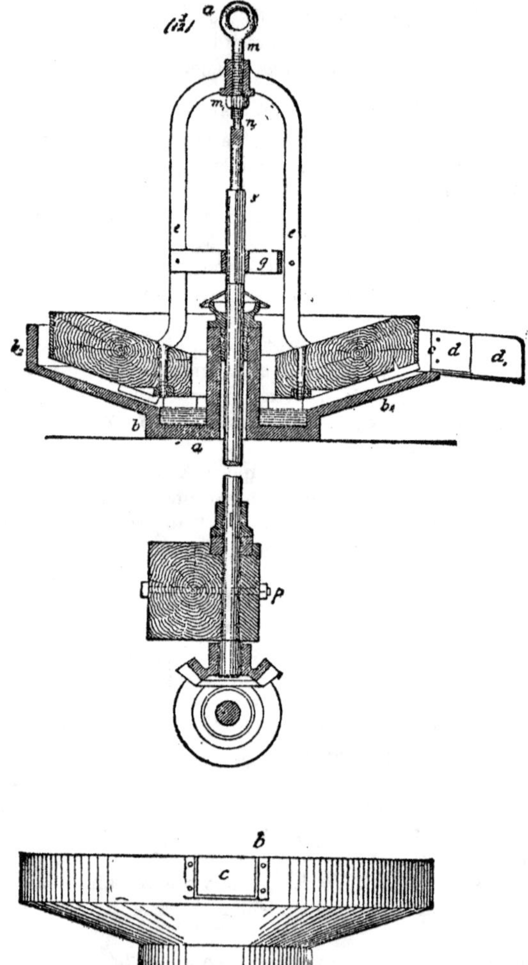

Figure 7.—The Austrian Gold Mill.

ore that contains much pyrites the former is best with ores very poor in pyrites, the latter.

Amalgamation takes place in pans, there called "mills," an illustration of which is given in figure 7.

In this figure *a* is the pan, *l* the runner, *e* the arms, three in number, by which the runner is fastened to the spindle, *s* is a brace which both stiffens the arms *e*, and also transmits the movement of the spindle to the arms. The spindle is made square at this point, and the aperture in the brace being also square, the brace, arms and runner are carried round by the revolution of the spindle. Discharge takes place at *c*, a spout of sheet iron *d* being rivetted to the cast-iron pan. The adjusting apparatus consists of the thumb-screw *m*. It is to be remarked that the spindle ends at *n*, the end being hollowed out to receive the end of the thumb-screw. This screw works in a thread, cut to receive it, in the top of the arms *e*. The spindle itself rests on the beam *p*, and cannot move up or down. When the thumbscrew *m* is turned, its bearing on the top of the spindle remains constant, but the arms and consequently the runner are raised or lowered.

The pan is made of cast-iron, and as it suffers little wear can be made very light. The arms, which, being three in number, form a tripod, are made of light bar iron, of about 1½ inches in width, and ¼ inch in thickness. The runner is of wood, having the shape of the mill, and hollowed out on top so as to form a hopper. It is bolted to the tripod, bound with ordinary hoop iron, and a number of short pieces of sheet-iron are driven into its lower surface. These "wings" are from 2½ to 3 inches long and ¾ inch wide, and act like the vanes in a fan blower, or rotary pump; that is, they force the pulp to partake of the rotary motion and drive it out of the machine. Twenty to thirty wings are placed radially in each runner, in such a manner as to break joints, from the center to the circumference. Those which work over the slanting part of the pan are made only one-half inch wide, in order to allow the wings placed over the mercury, freedom of motion. Other methods of gearing are also employed and pans are usually wider at the bottom than the figure represents. In this pan the interior of the bottom, where the mercury is placed, is only 9 inches in diameter; usually 15 inches in the width. As the center is taken up by the aperture through which the spindle passes, the real width of the annular space, filled with mercury, is in this pan only 3 inches, and in the ordinary pan 6½ inches. In both cases the diameter at the top is 24 inches, height 9 inches and the thickness ⅛-3-16 inch.

When pulp is poured into the runner, it passes through the center opening or eye, down to the mercury, where the action of the wings gives it a rotary motion, and at the same time carries it toward the circumference. These wings should revolve just above the mercury, but not in contact with it. By this means, every particle of the pulp passes part or all the way round the pan before it is discharged, and its path over the mercury is therefore longer. It does this with the least possible turbulence, and the gold particles have opportunity to reach the mercury, where, sinking in that fluid, they are safe from liability to be carried off on the stream.

Successful work depends upon the thickness of the pulp and the speed given the runner, and one of the advantages of this mill is the readiness with which its work can de altered to suit any kind or condition of ore.

Condition of the Pulp.—This depends upon two things, density and fineness. A concentrated ore has a much higher specific gravity than undressed ore, because the lighter minerals, quartz, etc., have been removed. The difference between its gravity and that of gold is therefore less, and we must take care, 1st to have the slime so thin that the gold particles will have easy movement through it; and 2nd that the motion of the runner shall be fast enough to keep the heavy material which it has to carry along, from settling on the surface of the mercury. Experience has proved that with undressed ore containing not more than 10 per cent. of heavy mineral (pyrites, etc.,) to 90 per cent. of gangue, the runner should make from 12 to 15 revolutions per minute; from one-half to one cubic foot of pulp may be passed every minute; and finally this pulp must be of such a thickness that not more than 125 pounds of ore shall pass through the the mill in one hour.

When the ore has been concentrated the conditions are quite different. The runner is revolved at the rate of 20 to 30 times a minute, and the pulp must be thinned so that not more than 13 to 15 pounds of ore pass through the mill hourly. The amount of pulp however must be kept up to a half or one cubic foot a minute.

If the pulp is too coarse it hangs back in the mill and chokes it, if it is too fine the gold does not settle. *Good* stamp work answers well. It is not well to suffer pulp to dry and then wet it to run through the mill. Experience proves that the extraction is not so good under such circumstances, probably because the particles of gold have air adhering to them which lessens their gravity.

Two or three mills are usually placed one after the other. With these, of the whole amount of gold extracted from a pulp rich in galena and therefore not favorable to amalgamation.

The first extracted	65	per cent.
The second	25	"
The third	10	"

With a sandy pulp which contained little heavy mineral the result was:

The first extracted	74	per cent.
The second	20	"
The third	6	"

One mill, or one set of 2 or 3 mills, will pass from 2,250 to 3,000 pounds of undressed pulp in 24 hours. Of dressed ore it will pass through about as much as would correspond to that quantity of unconcentrated pulp. When the ore contains 10 per cent. of heavy minerals there is no gain in previous concentration, while the extraction is better with undressed pulp.

In this apparatus loss of mercury is reduced to a minimum. With two rows of pans the loss for 100,000 pounds of

pulp rich in heavy mineral was	1·5 to 2 pounds
" poor " " "	1 to 1·5 pounds

In the first case it was therefore about one-half ounce to one ton; in the second one-third ounces. Clayey ores and those containing antimony increase this loss.

The yield can be increased by concentrating the amalgamated pulp, and repassing the tailings under the conditions necessary in working concentrated pulp. By this means from 20 to 30 per cent. of the lost mercury is recovered, while about the same amount of the amalgamable gold is also won. The first operation extracts about 70 per cent.

The power necessary to run one mill is about *one twenty-fith* of a horse power. A twelve pan apparatus costs in Austria about $250.

Compared with the Colorado methods, these mills extract 20 per cent. more than the Colorado amalgators, though this yield necessarily depends upon the per centage of silver in the native gold. They require little watching, except when used immediately after the stamps, when the accumulation of gold might necessitate cleaning up every two or three days.

Smelting.—For four years the ores delivered for fusion were in the following propoitions :—

	From Rauris.	From Boeckstein.
Quartzose ore	6.50	24.11
Compact pyrites	0.06	0.48
Sulphuret of Antimony	1.41	0.41
Slime from Amalgamation	29.03	38.00
	37.00	63.00

About 60 per cent. of the ore has therefore been amalgamated. As this was done because the ore was too poor to smelt we may gain an idea of the extreme poverty of the original ore.

From the table of values before given, it is evident that 70—75 per cent. of the ore is worthless rock, and this must be removed before adding lead, which would suffer serious loss if charged with so much quartz. The operations are therefore as follows :—

1. Fusion for raw matte.
2. Roasting of raw matte in stalls.
3. Fusion (without lead) for a more concentrated matte.
4. Roasting of 2nd matte in stalls.
5. Fusion with lead.
6. Cupellation of rich lead.

The First Fusion.—Eleven years experience has proved that the most efficient slag is one approaching the composition of a bisilicate. The following is an analysis of an average slag from the first fusion :—

Silica	51.02
Alumina	2.16
Oxide of Iron	19.75
Lime	15.40
Magnesia	8.57
As. Mn. Ca.	
Zn. S. by dif.	3.10
	100,000

The furnace is not new and contains none of the late improvements ; but it does good service. Its general dimensions are as follows :—

Height	24 feet.
Diameter of hearth	3 "
" boshes	4 "
" throat	2 "
Number of tuyeres	2 "
Pressure of blast	$\frac{1}{3}$—$\frac{1}{2}$ in. of mercury.

From 100 to 120 bushels of charcoal are required to warm the furnace, and then regular charges of 5 cubic feet, or about 3 bushels are thrown in. In blowing in, the quantity of mixed ore and flux added to this quantity of charcoal is, at first 56 pounds, then 112 pounds, and finally when the furnace is thoroughly hot, 203 pounds, which is the constant burden of mine to three bushels of charcoal. This is usually reached in the first 24 hours. Four hours after the first charge of ore and flux the blast is turned on, at first with a pressure of $\frac{1}{3}$ in., and then $\frac{1}{2}$ in. mercury; or one-sixth and one-quarter pounds pressure. After eight hours the slag begins to flow. The furnace is worked with a black throat. The labor per ton of ore and flux amounts to 1.8 days.

The First Matte, forms 40 to 45 per cent. of the charge, the difference between this proportion and the 20 to 30 per cent. afforded by the ore being made up by roasted matte which forms a part of the charge. Its average composition is:—

Iron	55.1
Copper	4.3
Zinc	3.7
Lead	2.1
Nickel, Cobalt, Arsenic and Antimony	4 5
Sulphur	27.9
	97.6

It contains 30 to 40 ounces Troy of auriferous silver to 2,000 pounds; or in American valuation $100 to $150 in coin. From the fact that the ore is unroasted, and the metals are therefore so well "covered" by sulphur, the loss in this operation amounts to only one-quarter of one per cent. About 38 bushels of charcoal are used to the ton of charge, and 9.75 tons are smelted in 24 hours.

The Second Fusion.—The first matte is roasted three times in stalls containing 28 tons, the roasting not being thorough, but carried only so far as to leave about 40 per cent. of unroasted matte. It is then resmelted with quartz, and to avoid the use of too much of the latter, a basic slag is made containing about 22 per cent. silica. This requires very great care in managing the furnace, for the least irregularity will cause the formation of sows. To secure proper working, whenever the furnace is tapped, the hearth is examined by means of a bent bar. If lumps are felt the front wall is broken out, and they are removed; if the sole is slippery the presence of reduced iron is indicated. A rough, hard, even sole, is the proper one.

The pressure of blast is now reduced to one-sixth of an inch or one-twelfth of a pound to the square inch; the hearth is 10 to 12 inches larger in diameter than before, and the charge is increased to 222 pounds to 3 bushels of charcoal. These changes have for their object not only the prevention of iron sows but also of speise, a compound of arsenic with all the other metals, very difficult to utilize.

Speise is lighter than matte, and in the basin lies next above it. That at Lend contains a great deal of gold, and experiments made a few years ago to recover this metal by roasting and fusion with lead were not successful, though the speise was roasted in 8 to 12 fires and smelted with twice its weight of lead. It was found nearly impossible to oxidize all the speise and the unroasted part retained its gold with stubbornness. The same precautions are used in blowing in as before. About 30 bushels of charcoal are used to the ton of ore and flux, and 13.5 tons are fused in 24 hours. The second matte, contains 50 to 60 ounces of auriferous silver to 2,000 pounds, worth about $200.

Fusion with Lead.—The second matte is roasted as before, but now 50 to 60 per cent. of raw matte is left. A stronger roasting would so enrich it that two fusions with lead instead of one, would be necessary. The slag is again basic and, to keep the heat as low as possible, the pressure of blast is reduced to one and one-half lines of mercury, while the charge is increased to 277 pounds of matte and flux to 3 bushels of charcoal. In order to keep the lead in contact with the matte as long as possible, as well as to decrease the heat, the crucible is made a foot deeper than before. The new slag has an average composition of

Silica	27.45
Oxide of Iron	56.52
Lime	10.19
Magnesia	3.48
Alumina	1.25

The loss will not exceed 2.5 per cent. of the lead. When the hearth is full of melted matte and lead, it is tapped, the products running into a basin where they are well stirred with poles. The matte is then partially taken off, the lead remaining until 600 to 700 pounds has collected.

For a perfect extraction of the silver, it is necessary to charge 120 to 130 pounds of lead for each pound of silver and gold, and the matte must not contain more than 20 per cent. copper. With this proportion, 75 per cent. of the silver and gold are extracted in one operation, and the matte ought not to contain more than 0.75 per cent. of lead. The extraction of 75 per cent. of auriferous silver, means that 90 per cent. of the gold and 73 per cent. of the silver has been obtained. The absolute loss of these metals is but 0.10 of one per cent. From 14 to 16 tons are smelted in 24 hours. A certain amount of lead matte is obtained which is charged back in the same operation. Of charcoal, 28 bushels to the ton are used. If the matte is rich enough, it now undergoes a repetition of this operation, but usually it is so poor that it is treated immediately for copper. If, however, it contains less than 35 per cent. of copper, it is roasted and charged as a flux, in the first operation for raw matte. At Lend the conditions are such that this takes place every other year, copper being made one year and matte the next. The labor amounts to 0.46 days per ton of matte and flux, and the loss of lead is about 18 pounds to the ton of matte.

Cupellation is performed in a German furnace with a moveable hood, made very low. Inasmuch as none of the side products are sold, and there is no need of having them in great purity, there is beside the fire bridge, but one opening in the hearth, through which abzug, abstrich, litharge and smoke all escape. From

6,000 to 7,000 pounds of lead are first charged, and more is gradually added until about 21,000 pounds (or the entire make for the year) has been melted. The blast is slow, and the litharge consequently flows rather cold. Refining follows the brightening of the silver, and metal of 985 fineness is produced. Usually the loss of lead falls between 5 and 6 per cent., while that of silver and gold seldom reaches 0.10 per cent. About 3 tons are cupelled in 24 hours, and the labor is 0.24 days per ton.

TABLES OF THE OPERATIONS.

The following tables will give at a glance all the foregoing particulars. The first two operations are combined in one table, and instead of calculating the expense of charcoal upon the quantity of material treated in each operation, that and the amount of labor will be calculated upon the ton of ore. This is done in order to ascertain how much labor and fuel are necessary to treat a ton of ore by the Lend process. The amount of ore is taken at 109 tons since there was 21 tons of matte remaining from the previous year which was smelted with the ore.

TABLE OF THE 1ST AND 2ND FUSIONS, 1866.

Charge	*Weight Tons.*	*Ounces of Gold.*	*Ounces of Silver.*	*p. c. of Copper.*
Ore	81·15	21·0094	1333·4058	
Matte and Rich Scraps	89·61	19·2918	2216·6406	
Flux { Basic 7.41 / Siliceous 50.88	59 29			
Total	229·05	40·3012	3550·0464	
Products.				
First Matte	61·38	18·7193	1612·7324	5
Second Matte	30·87	20·4769	1806·7302	10
Scraps	10·25	·6824	95·0922	
Total		39.8776	3514·5548	

Labor 39 twelve hour shifts ; 5 men to each shift = 195 days.

Charcoal for warming furnace, 291 bushels.
" for smelting, 6,820 "

7,111 "

Charcoal per ton of ore....... 65·2 bushels
Labor per ton of ore...... ...... 1.8 days.

TABLE OF THIRD FUSION, 1866.

Charge.		Tons.	Lead. Pounds.	Copper. Per ct.	Gold. Troy ounces.	Silver. Troy ounces.
Containing Gold and Silver.	Rich quartzose ore...	1·96			0·9610	59·5404
	Roasted 2d Matte....	30·87		10	20·4769	1806·7202
	Scraps..............	2·09			·1474	23·0778
Containing Lead.	Lead Matte..........	3·71	741	6	1·9440	175 9600
	Litharge.............	10·81	17,722			66·1500
	Hearth..............	3·30	3,304			42·4700
Flux.	Slag from 1st Fusion...	10·99				
	Quartz...............	2·04				
		66·77			23·5293	2175·9184
Products.						
Lead.....................		10·51	21,030		21·5442	1283·8320
Third Matte..................		15·59				624·5200
Lead Matte..................		3·70	741	20	1·9440	174·9600
Scraps and Flue Dust.........		4·06		10	0·2430	46·9900
					23 7312	2130.2920

Labor 10 twelve hour shifts ; 5 men in each—50 days.

Charcoal for warming the furnace..........	100	bushels.
" " smelting....................	1710	"
	1810	"
Labor per ton of ore..................	0·46	days.
Charcoal "	16·6	bushels.
Lead charged "	218	pounds.

TABLE OF CUPELLATION.

Charged.	*Tons.*	*Lead p. c.*	*Gold. Troy ounces.*	*Silver. Troy ounces.*
Lead....................	10.06	100	21·5442	1283·8320
Products.				
Fine Silver...............	1208·58 oz.		21·5294	1186 9560
Litharge.................	10 tons	82		64·9080
Hearth..................	2·53 "	50		31·9860
Loss..			0·0144	
Gain..				0.1800

Labor, 26 days = per ton of ore............	0.24	days.
Wood, 7·52 cords. "	0·69	cords.
Charcoal, 40·00 bushels = per ton of ore....	0·37	bushels.

TABLE OF COST PER TON OF ORE IN UNITS OF LABOR AND MATERIAL.

	Labor. Days.	Charcoal. Bushels.	Wood. Cords.	Lead. Pds.
First and Second Fusion..............	1.8	65·2	—	—
Third Fusion..........................	0·46	16·6	—	8·0
Cupellation...........................	0·24	0·37	0·69	9.7
Total....................	2·50	82·17	0·69	17·7

To this must be added a small quantity of wood or refuse charcoal, used in roasting the matte. Some discrepancies will be noticed between the expense of charcoal as given in these tables and that allotted to each operation in the text. This arises from the fact that the latter is calculated upon the proportions of flux and ore, while the tables are calculated upon the ore alone. They are also more complete: including fuel, for blowing in, blowing out, and any extra supplies needed in particular states of the furnace. The quantity of charcoal has been calculated on the heaped bushel of 2,748 cubic inches. The above cost is for ores of the richness before given. With richer ores there is more matte to treat and lead lost, and the cost is therefore somewhat greater per ton; but it is proportionately less per pound of gold and silver. The following table gives the relative cost for various ores; the cost of the poorest being taken as unity:—

Auriferous Silver in 2000 Lbs.	*Value in American Coin.*	*Proportionate Cost; lowest taken as Unity.*
0— 14·5. oz.	$ 0—$ 61	1
14·5— 29·0	$ 61—$122	1·10
29·0— 58·0	$122—$244	1 31
58·0—116·0	$244—$488	1·73

The Lend ore falls under the first kind; the milling ore of Colorado is worth from $20 to $30 a ton, and therefore is also in the lowest section; the "smelting ore," so called, would be mostly in the 2nd and 3d ranks.

LOSSES.—By reference to the above tables it will be found that the following is the loss and gain of the year.

	Loss.				Gain.			
	Gold.		Silver.		Gold.		Silver.	
	oz.	p. c.	oz.	p. c.	oz.	p. c.	oz.	p. c.
First and Second Fusions......	4·24	1	35·50	2·8				
Third Fusion..................	—	—	45 63	3·6	2·029	0.86		
Cupellation	0 15	0.07					0·02	0·0015
	4·39		81·13		2·029		0·02	
Total loss..............	2·36	1·1	81·11	6·2				

Dr. Turner's opinion founded upon years of experience, is that more than 90 per cent. of the silver and 96 per cent. of the gold can be counted upon in the two processes of amalgamation and fusion. Some years ago he undertook to ascertain the loss incurred in amalgamating and found it to be 45 per cent. He therefore placed no reliance upon his results, but when we consider the poverty of the milling ore, we shall see that a loss of one half the gold contained in it would affect but very little the grand result.

The cost of all the operations in 1866, at Lend, was $883.88, and the balance sheet shows a profit of $1,355. The expense was proportioned as follows : Labor 17, materials 43, direction 40 ; total 100.

At these works all avoidable causes of loss have been eliminated, or their operation reduced with the greatest care. Two analyses a year determine the proportions of the charges and the composition of the slag. Larger works would require more, but there is no reason why the largest works should not be conducted with equal care.

Great care is necessary on account of the extremely small quantity of ore smelted ; —only 83 tons in 1866, worth less than $2260 in gold and silver, but furnishing also a ton and a half of copper. But to treat this small quantity an engineer, and two smelters and four assistants have to be supported all the year through, though they work only 27 days of 24 hours. Of course such a state of things can be maintained only by low prices, and we find the Austrian workmen paid at rates varying from 27½ to 22 cents (coin) a day. Charcoal is 3 1-7 cents a bushel, and wood $1 17 a cord. In this country we should have larger supplies of ore, sufficient to carry on the largest works on a correspondingly economical scale. The nature and higher value of our ores, too, would enable us to work with less expense of labor and material to the Troy pound of gold and silver than at Lend.

In considering these results for guidance in using a similar process at the West it is evident that the American ores contain nothing to prevent the application of this process. Antimony and arsenic and zinc, the bugbears of the smelter, are, with the exception perhaps of zinc, quite as prevalent at Lend as in Colorado, Our ores, too, contain more pyrites than those we have been considering and there would be no necessity for a fusion for raw matte. Whether there ought to be a fusion for concentration depends upon the richness of the ore, and its adaptability to concentration by machinery. A mixture of rich "smelting ore" and concentrated tailings, such as is now worked up by the smelters, could be roasted and immediately fused with lead. One more fusion with a fresh quantity of lead and cupellation would complete the process. We should then have a process divided as follows :

1. Cupellation of poor ore.
2. Roasting of concentrated and rich ore.
3. Fusion of roasted ore with lead.
4. Roasting of matte.
5. Fusion of matte with lead.
6. Cupellation,

As to the cost of a process like this, we have the following details. A ton of concentrated tailings is produced in Colorado at an average cost of $6. The expenses for the other 5 operations would be :

	Day's labor.	Charcoal.	Wood.
Roasting in Piles	0·4		0·029 cords.
1st and 2nd Fusions	1·8	65·2	
Roasting matte	0·2		0·004
Third Fusion	0·46	16·6	
Cupellation	0·24	00·37	0·69
	10	82·17	0·720

Mr. Hague says that the millers expect to get one ton of concentrated tailings from six tons of ore. At that basis the theoretical expense would be:

Concentrating 6 tons to one...............................	$ 6 00
Smelting 1 ton, 3·10 days labor @ $3................	9 30
Smelting 1 ton, 82·17 bushels charcoal @ 25c.........	20 54
Smelting 0·72 cords wood @ $8.......................	6 00
Treatment of 6 tons milling ore......................	41 84
Mining of 6 tons milling ore @ $10..................	60 00
Total cost of treatment..............................	101 84
Cost of one ton..................................	16 94

The expense of charcoal ought to be somewhat less than this, for in consequence of the small quantity of material treated at Lend no less than 2.5 bushels of coal to a ton of ore are expended in heating the furnace. If we add one half more for loss in blowing out we have the very large proportion of 3.7 bushels, a quantity that would be lessened one bushel if 330 tons of ore were smelted at each campaign. With proper management this could be very much exceed d so that the expense of charcoal for blowing in and blowing out, would be too small per ton to be worth reckoning.

It now remains to consider the adaptability of this process to western ores, and I will take those of Colorado as an example, for the reason that Mr. Hague's report on mines of that Territory offers the best data for calculation. He gives commercial assays of the ore from various lodes which prove the average value of the ores to be as follows:

First class ore:	Gold.	Silver.
Consolidated Gregory.............	5.6 oz.	20 oz.
Illinois.............................	4	20
Gardner...........................	3.5	11.5
California.........................	3.	18
Burroughs.........................	6.	12
Average...........................	4.42	16.3
Milling ore:		
Burroughs (1340 tons)............	1 oz.	4.5 oz.

The value of the first class ore is $91.36 for the gold and $21.03 for the silver; total $112.13. Let us see what manipulation it requires: Roasting the ore so as to leave 33 per cent raw matte, and smelting with 180 to 195 pounds of lead to the ton of ore we ought to extract in one operation 93 per cent. of the gold, or 4.05 ounces worth $83.71; and 73 per cent. of the silver or 11.90 ounces worth $15.-35; total yield $99.05.(4) The expense of working would be as follows:

(4) By reference to the tables of cupellation and loss it will be seen that in 1866 more than 99 per cent. of the gold was obtained by one fusion with lead; while of the silver 60 per cent. was obtained as metal, and 32 per cent. was retained by the third matte and went under treatment the following year, 2.4 per cent. was contained in the scraps and flue dust, 3.3 per cent. was retained by the litharge. The latter two should be neglected for they are constant from year to year, and the real percentage yield was in 1866, therefore, 63·8 per cent. fine silver, and 33·9 per cent. silver in the matte.

Mining—1 ton			$10 00
Roasting—0.4 days labor @ $3	$1 20		
0.029 cords wood @ $8	0 23		
8 mos. int. on $10 @ 12 p. c.	80	2 23	
Smelting—1.5 days labor @ $3	4 50		
8 pounds lead @ 5c	40		
46 bushels charcoal @ 25c	11 50	16 40	18 63
Total for mining and smelting			28 63

If our ore contains no copper the matte will not pay for further treatment and we proceed at once to cupellation, for which we have in addition:

Cupellation: 0.24 days labor at $3	$0 75	
0.37 bushels coal at 25c	09	
0.69 cords wood at $8	5 52	
9 lbs of lead at 5c	45	6 81
Add mining and smelting		28 63
		$35 44

Profit: $99 06—$35 44=$63 62.

We have remaining a matte containing $7 48. Let us see whether this will pay to work by itself. The expense will be for Colorado rather greater than for Lend because the proportion of pyrites in the ore is greater. Assuming this excess equal to 50 per cent. and increasing each item to that extent we have:

Roasting: 0.50 days labor at $3	$0 90	
0.2 cords wood at $8	18	1 08
Smelting: 0.60 days labor at $3	1 80	
27 bushels of coal at 25c	6 75	
5 pounds lead at 5c	25	9 80
Total		$10 88

This would leave a loss; $7 48—$10 88=*minus* $3 40. The loss by direct treatment would therefore be $3 40. This matte however could be returned to the first fusion again and again, until the copper which is present to some extent in almost all the ores were concentrated sufficiently to give the matte a value for its copper. With ores containing much copper the matte might be immediately saleable, and both silver and copper bring their value. At present however, and especially with milling ores, the process would probably consist of three stages, as follows:

1. Roasting.
2. Fusion with lead.
3. Cupellation.

To illustrate the working of the process with milling ore, let us take the Burroughs ore as a specimen. It is worth one ounce gold, or $20 67, and 4 5 oz. silver, or $5 80; total $26 47. This is an average yield, as most of the milling ore of Colorado, so far treated, lies between $18 and $35 in value. We have for its treatment by fusion the following expenses:

FREIBERG.

ALTHOUGH the processes in use at Freiberg have been described with tolerable frequency, few persons who are not instructed in schools of mines, have a just appreciation of the works there, or a correct idea of the methods in use. Those methods, in fact, change so constantly that it would require a year-book to keep pace with them. They have changed so much since 1870, that in writing the following description, the work of later travellers, such as Messrs. KAST, BRAUNING and KUHLEMANN, all of them connected with the great works in the Hartz Mountains, and BALLING, of the Austrian service, have been freely drawn upon.

After more than 500 years' exploitation, the mines of Freiberg form a vast network of galleries and drifts. Within the century ending in 1865 a total length of 25 German miles, or 115 English miles of passages was excavated and the mines were deepened 700—900 feet. What the cubic contents amounted to is not known, but it is surmised from the number of men employed in 1765, (1255, of whom probably not more than 600 were engaged in breaking down), that about 19,200 cubic yards or 5,539 cords, of 128 cubic feet, of rock was taken out in that year. The amount excavated in 1865 was 128,206 cubic yards or 59,190 cords, which gives close on 8 cords per German *Lachter* (6 2-3 feet) of excavation. At the same rate the excavation for 100 years past would average 36,969 cords per year. It is a matter of interest to know that in 1765 a cord of rock gave 1 ton of concentrated ore; while in 1865 a cord of rock gave only 66-100ths of a ton. Baron VON BEUST, however, does not ascribe this falling off to a regular decrease of the ore in depth, nor to the fact that the dressing works now accept poorer ores from the miner than then, though this probably has some effect; but rather to the very large works for drainage and improvement of communication, most of which are done in dead rock, outside of the veins, and (chiefly) to the fact, of which he is persuaded, that the Freiberg mines now and for some years back, have been worked in one of those zones of medium and poor ore which occur in all veins. According to this view these famous mines should have before them a renewal of their former extreme wealth when this poor zone has been worked through.

More than 900 veins are known, which have been classed, according to the ores they yield, in four groups:

1. The quartz group, containing about 150 veins, from 3 inches to 6 or 7 feet wide. This would probably be called in America the *silver* group, for its valuable mineral consists mostly of various silver minerals. The gangue is quartz with some gneiss, and the ores are silver glance, ruby silver, fahlerz, miargyrite, polybasite, brittle silver ore, antimony glance and antimony sulphide.

2. The pyritiferous group, with about 300 veins, of 2 inches to 3 feet width. The gangue is chiefly quartz, with some calc-spar, iron-spar, heavy-spar and fluor-spar. The principal ores are argentiferous galena, blende, pyrites, arsenical pyrites, with a certain proportion of the minerals named in connection with the first group. To this group belong also the veins which yield chiefly copper ores; as copper pyrites, peacock ore, copper glance, red oxide and carbonate of copper.

3. The noble lead group, so-called from its richer ores, has 340 veins, in which the gangue is brown spar, manganese spar and quartz. The ores are galena, richer in silver than that of the preceding division, blende, pyrites, native silver and some proper silver minerals.

4. The barytic lead group, with 130 veins, some of them very wide. The gangue is heavy spar, with some fluor-spar and quartz, and the ores are galena, blende and pyrites, with some carbonates and silver minerals.

The ores obtained from these extensive mines may be briefly described as containing *all* the lead, silver and copper minerals, that are not mere cabinet curiosities, besides most of those that are such. The total quantity delivered in 1867, was 34,163 tons (2,000 lbs.) which contained by assay:

			Per Cent.	In 1 Ton.
71,444·25	pounds	silver and gold	= 0·104	30·47 ounces.
5,130·00	tons	lead	= 15·01	300·20 pounds.
78·75	"	copper	= 0·23	4·60 pounds.
664·25	"	zinc	= 1·94	38·80 pounds.
174·50	"	arsenic	= 0·51	11·20 pounds.

There are two establishments at Freiberg, the Muldner and Halsbrücke Works. Differences in the composition of the ores have given rise to slight deviations in treatment, and for the sake of consistency this paper will deal with the course of operations at the Muldner Works alone, while that in use at Halsbrücke will not be referred to, except in describing the copper treatment which is carried on only there.

The Muldner Works treated in 1867, 16,702 tons of ore and furnace products, which contained by assay:

			Per Cent.	In 1 Ton.	
43,197·45	Av. pounds	silver	0·129	37·62	Troy oz.
106·89	"	gold	0·00032	0·093	"
4o4·41	"	bismuth	0·0014	0·03	pounds.
608·88	"	nick'l & cobalt	0·0018	0·04	"
7,520,704·00	"	lead	22·51	450·02	"
137,445·90	"	copper	0·41	8·20	"
7,702,546 63	or	3,851 tons.			

By comparing this table with that above given, it will be observed that the ore treated at the Muldner Works appears to be richer than the great average. This is because a great amount of furnace products are added to the ore, because nearly all the foreign ores are taken to this establishment, which lies immediately on the railroad, while the other works is several miles from it. These foreign ores are much richer than the average Freiberg ore, as the fact that they are able to bear a transportation of several thousand miles, and still afford a profit, indicates.

The total amount of these products, according to the table, is 3,851 tons, or very nearly 25 per cent. Seventy-five per cent. of the ore is therefore material which must be removed. This material is of two kinds, useful, as sulphur and arsenic; and worthless, as quartz and other gangue. The useful constituents are economised as much as possible, and this gives rise to a series of operations which are supplementary to the regular course of smelting.

Thirteen different products are obtained as follows:

Metals.	Products.
1 Gold.	1 Sulphuric acid.
2 Silver.	2 Copper vitriol.
3 Lead.	3 Arsenic, white and yellow.
4 Zinc.	4 Orpiment, or arsenic sulphide.
5 Arsenic.	5 Speise, containing cobalt and nickel.
6 Bismuth.	6 Zinc paint.
7 Platinum.	

The process is, however, *primarily* one for the extraction of lead and copper, with their accompanying gold and silver, the rest being all bye products. Certain preliminary operations have to be undertaken in order to prepare the ores containing arsenic, sulphur and zinc, but holding no lead, for the fusion with lead ores in which they part with their silver. These preliminary steps have been grouped together in the following paper in a PREPARATORY SERIES of operations. Then follows the REGULAR SERIES, in which all the operations connected with the fusion of the lead ores and the extraction of the silver, gold and copper, are placed. Finally, in a SUPPLEMENTARY SERIES, are given the operations in which marketable articles are prepared, not from ores, but from various products obtained during the course of the previous work.

Only by keeping in mind the fact, that there is one leading series of operations, which has for its object the production of lead, silver, gold and copper, and upon which all the other work is dependent, can a clear idea of the varied methods in use at Freiberg, be obtained.

The processes placed in these three series are as follows:

Preparatory.	Regular.	Supplementary.
Manufacture of Arsenic.	Fusions for Lead.	Bismuth Process.
" " Sulphuric Acid.	Treatment of Matte.	Hard Lead Process.
" " Zinc.	Cupellation.	Separation of Gold.
" " Zinc Paint.	Treatment of Copper.	Manuf. Platinum.
	Treatment of Lead.	Refining Arsenic.

Seven sorts of ore are recognized:

1. Pyrites; iron pyrites containing not more than 1 per cent. copper, or 15 per cent. zinc, and little arsenic.
2. Arsenic ores; averaging 35 per cent. metallic arsenic.
3. Arsenical pyrites; 15 per cent. arsenic, 26—28 per cent. sulphur.
4. Arsenical lead ores; 12 per cent arsenic, 18—20 per cent. lead.
5. Blende; with more than 30 per cent. zinc.
6. Pyritiferous ores; containing 15—30 per cent. zinc.
7. Lead ores; 1, galena, with more than 30 per cent. lead, and 2, plumbiferous ore, with 15—29 per cent. lead.

But following the system pursued in this paper, the old classification into fluxes, lead ores, dry ores and copper ores, will be retained. The fluxes are in the main those which contain so much iron as to make them valuable additions to the fusion for lead. They are chiefly iron pyrites containing arsenic and zinc; but the zinc ores also belong in this class, the residues after the distillation of the zinc being carried to the lead process and added in the roasting furnace. The dry ores (Dürrerze), are so called from the absence of lead. In this country they would be called distinctively *silver* ores, for their valuable part consists of true silver minerals. They are worked with the lead ores in the shaft furnace, and therefore come in the regular series. But if their quantity is too great to be disposed of in this way, they can be melted in a reverberatory with slag from the fusion for lead, and then belong to the preparatory series. This was formerly the basis of the Freiberg treatment. Now it is, at most, an exceptional operation.

PREPARATORY SERIES OF OPERATIONS.

Roasting:—Chief among these operations is roasting, or the removing of the sulphur. For this, four varieties of furnace are used: 1. kilns; 2. Gerstenhöfer furnaces; 3. Wellner's stalls; 4. reverberatory furnaces. The first two are connected with the sulphuric acid chambers. Kilns are used for ore in lumps, and for matte. Those in which ore is roasted are 10 feet high, and 7×5 feet in section; those for matte are 10 feet high, and 10×5 feet in section, the long side in both cases forming the front. They have numerous small side openings through which the workmen can observe and regulate the operation. The charge for the larger furnaces is 1,760 to 2,200 pounds, and for the smaller 650 to 1,300 pounds. A charge is drawn every twelve hours, so that one kiln roasts in twenty-four hours, of matte 3,500—4,400 pounds, and of ore 1,300—2,600 pounds. No fuel is used. The sulphur is reduced to 8 per cent. When it is necessary to roast the coarse ore or matte more thoroughly, Wellner's stalls are employed. These have grates upon which a fire is maintained, by which the sulphur is more thoroughly removed than can be done by any heat produced by its own combustion. But as sulphur is needed in the shaft furnace, the re-roasting of these coarse ores is rather exceptional.

For fine ores, the Gerstenhöfer furnace is employed for preliminary roasting. The form of this, as is well known, is that of an upright shaft containing triangular bricks, reaching from side to side, the upper surfaces of which form shelves on which the ore periodically rests. These furnaces have not answered the expectations formed of them, and they are retained at Freiberg more as the best construction in some respects that has yet been devised for finely crushed ores, than as a thorough roasting apparatus. They do not reduce the sulphur beyond 12 or 13 per cent., and are used as a preparation for reverberatories. The roasting is not always uniform; but for fine ore, they are almost the only resort of the smelter, who wishes to utilize his sulphur in the manufacture of sulphuric acid.

Roasting only to 13 per cent., these furnaces require to be supplemented by reverberatories an interesting variety of which is found at Freiberg. They are all long furnaces, the ore gradually advancing from the cool to the hot end. Three kinds are in use, double hearth furnaces of 47 and of 76 feet hearth length, and single hearth furnaces ; both sizes of the former have upper hearths of the width of 6 feet and lower hearths of 5 feet 6 inches. It was found that the shorter furnaces did their work just as well as the longer, in less time and with less labor. In building a new furnace, it was therefore made of 47 feet hearth length, the upper hearth 7 feet wide and the lower 6 feet 6 inches. These double hearth furnaces, and especially the old forms, which have a flue on top, are extremely hard to keep in repair ; and trial was made at the Halsbrücke works, of a single hearth furnace, 48 feet long and 10 feet wide. This gives more hearth room than the longest of the old furnaces, and allows doors to be made on both sides ; while the two-banked furnaces mostly have doors on one side only, a disposition which makes it very difficult to move ore that lodges between the doors. This furnace roasts fully as well as the older forms, and also disposes of about 50 per cent. more material.

The Gerstenhöfer furnaces and the kilns are connected with a system of flues, in which the arsenic, which forms a constituent of almost all the pyrites, is condensed. From the flues the sulphurous acid vapors pass to the lead chambers, where sulphuric acid is made. This condensation system is peculiar in having canals next the acid chambers, formed of sheet lead, by which the gas is so much cooled as to insure the most thorough precipitation of the arsenic. The gas also reaches the chambers in the best condition for condensation. The reverberatory furnaces have a special system of canals, in which a dust, very rich in arsenic, collects. As the gas is not utilizable for sulphuric acid, the canals end in a high chimney. With this description of the means for roasting, we will pass to the treatment of the various sorts of ore which are subjected to it.

Pyrites :—The coarse ore is roasted in kilns to about 8 per cent , and if desired, it is re-roasted in stalls. The fine ore first passes through the Gerstenhöfer furnace, in which the sulphur is reduced to 13 per cent., and is then mixed with the lead ores for roasting in a reverberatory.

Arsenic ores are of three kinds. 1. True arsenic ores ; 2. Arsenical pyrites ; and 3. Arsenical lead ores. The true arsenic ores are treated both for metallic arsenic, of which they contain about 35 per cent., and for arsenic sulphide. The operation consists in a distillation in chamotte tubes, first at a low temperature which drives over the arsenic sulphide, and then at a high heat, when the metallic arsenic passes over. The first collects in the extreme end of the condensing apparatus, and the second in that part nearest the furnace.

Arsenic sulphide is also obtained from the arsenical pyrites and from sulphuric acid residues. The former contain about 15 per cent. arsenic and 26—28 per cent. sulphur. This distillation is also performed in tubes. The residues still containing arsenic. are treated like the lead ores described in the next paragraph.

Arsenical lead ores are roasted in a reverberatory furnace, which has a hearth 14 feet long and 10 feet wide. In order to prevent the passage of sparks and soot into the flues where the arsenic condenses, the ordinary fir place is replaced by a simple gas generator. This is formed by merely sinking the grate about 3½ feet below the firebridge, and in the shaft thus produced coke is burned. Combustion takes place only in the lower part of the coke column, and the upper part is not heated sufficiently to decrepitate. The charge is about 2,000 pounds, which is roasted in six hours, at an expense of 275—330 pounds coke ; each furnace has a special flue 800 feet long, in which a perfectly white dust, free from soot, and suitable for the market, collects.

Zinc ores consist of blende, which is roasted with great care in reverberatories, by which the amount of sulphur is reduced to one and a half per cent. The roasted ore is then distilled in Silesian muffles, and the residues from the distillation are mixed with the roasted pyritiferous ores, and treated as described in the next paragraph. These residues contain 9—12 per cent. zinc; 1—2 per cent. copper; and 0·03—0.04 per cent. (8·7—11·6 ounces) silver.

Pyritiferous ores are pyrites containing blende. They have from 15—29 per cent. of zinc; 1—2 per cent. copper; 0·015—0·045 per cent. silver; and more than 20 per cent. of sulphur. Their treatment is one of the most peculiar in the whole range of metallurgy. It is impossible to utilize the zinc they contain as metal, and yet it must be eliminated, if the ore is to be charged in the fusion for lead, where a high percentage of zinc would seriously disturb the operation. The ore is, therefore, powdered fine, and roasted first in a Gerstenhöfer furnace. Residues from the zinc distillation are then added, and the whole is roasted in a reverberatory. The roasted ore is then mixed with coke slack and brown coal, and smelted at a high heat in a reverberatory furnace. The zinc oxide which has been formed in roasting, is now reduced to metal and volatilized, but immediately oxidizes again in the air, and collects in the flues in the form of a gray dust. This operation is conducted at a nearly white heat. About two-thirds the zinc is removed in this way, and the product—called dezincing residue—contains all the iron and not quite one-third the zinc of the original charge. The regular charge consists of

30 roasted ore; | 1·3 brown coal; | 1·6 coke slack.

From four to six charges are fused in twenty-four hours; and the expense of fuel, according to the average of five days run in September, 1869, was: For reduction 11·5; on the grate 30·8; total 42·3 per cent.

Products:

Residues=0·012 per cent (3½ oz.) silver, 8—10 per cent. zinc.

Speise, usually amounting to 4 per cent. of the ore. It contains 0·18 per cent. (5.2 oz.) silver, 2 per cent. lead, and 10 per cent. copper.

Lead is sometimes produced. It is very impure, forms about 0.16 per cent. of the ore, and contains 1·3 per cent. (389 oz.) silver.

Flue dust, which forms about 10 per cent. of the ore, and contains 0·005 per cent. (1½ oz.) silver, 10 per cent. lead, 24 per cent. zinc, and 30 per cent. sulphuric acid. The dust near the furnace contains a great deal of sulphuric acid. It is lixiviated and the residues returned to the furnace. The remainder is sold as paint.

The furnace in which this and similar operations are performed is an adaptation of that used in the English copper process. It is a reverberatory, in which the lining is composed of a mixture of sand, clay, and slag, sand alone, or any other material that may be desirable. A foundation of suitable size is dug out and lined with masonry. Small pillars of masonry (*c c*, Figures 7, 8, and 9) are also carried up nearly to the hearth level. On these strips of iron plate are laid, on which rests a number of iron plates, *b b* forming the hearth bottom. Upon these is placed a layer of broken stone *m*, then comes a layer of quartz and chamotte (old bricks ground up) *n*, and on this the hearth sole, *k*, made up usually of quartz and slag, is melted. The other parts of the furnace are : *d*, outer walls

Figure 9.

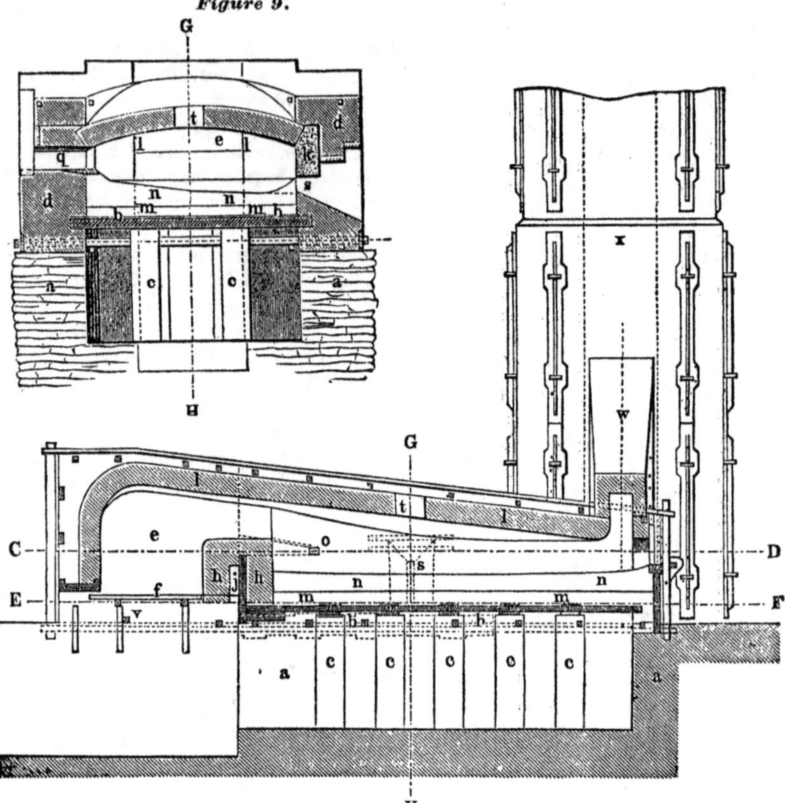

Figure 7.—Reverberatory Furnace at Freiberg.

of hard burned brick ; *e*, fire-place ; *f*, grate ; *g* fire door ; *h*, fire bridge of refractory brick ; *j*, opening in fire bridge to cool it ; *l*, arch made of refractory brick ; *o*, openings for admission of air ; *p*. working door ; *q* and *r*, side doors ; *s*, tap hole ; *t*, charging hole in roof ; *u* and *v*, supports for the tools ; *w*, the flue ; and *x*, the chimney, made of hard burned red brick, cemented with a mixture of quartz and clay. The whole is strongly bound with wrought-iron bars. Fig. 7 is a vertical side section, Fig. 8 a horizontal section and Fig. 9 an end section of the furnace.

This operation is not one to be imitated except under peculiar circumstances, for it is so costly and its product of so little value, that the proceeds hardly more than cover expenses. At Freiberg, it is valuable for other reasons than pecuni ary profit. One of the greatest defects of the Freiberg ore was formerly its lack of iron, a want which was one of the reasons that in former times led to the adoption of a reverberatory furnace process, after a trial of the shaft furnace had failed. Freiberg produces iron pyrites mixed with zinc, but this source of iron was useless until this method of eliminating m'st of the zinc, was discovered. To merely roast the ore and add it to the charge in the shaft furnace would cause the entrance of so much zinc into the slag that it would be both pasty

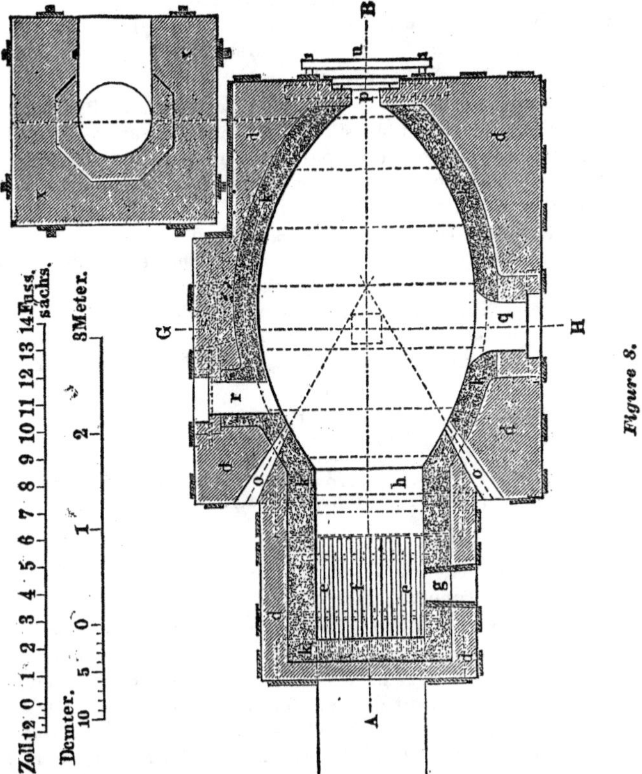

Figure 8.

and nearly infusible. But by distilling the zinc off, a residue rich in iron and comparatively poor in zinc, is obtained; and this forms a very acceptable addition to the lead ores.

REGULAR SERIES OF OPERATIONS.

From all the above operations we have the following products :

1. From Sulphur ores—Roasted iron pyrites containing some lead, copper and silver.

2. From Arsenic ores—Roasted residues, having in the main the composition of roasted iron pyrites and still containing a certain proportion of arsenic, together with lead, copper and silver.

3. From Zinc ores—Dezincing residues, forming a slag, which contains much iron, 8—10 per cent. zinc, with lead, copper and silver; also a speise containing very much arsenic with iron, copper, lead, cobalt and nickel.

Besides these, the following ores remain for treatment: 1. Galena ores. 2. Lead bearing ores; (the average of the two is barely 40 per cent. lead and 0.15 per cent., (43¾ oz.) silver.) 3. Copper ores. 4 Dry ores.

The treatment now becomes that known as the Roasting and Reduction process; the ores being first roasted to a silicate and then reduced in the shaft furnace. In the former operation various purchased materials containing gold and silver, together with the residues from arsenic glass are added, and the products mentioned above serve as flux in the blast furnace. It is for this reason that the ores from which they have been obtained have received the name *Fluxes.* The first step is to make the "ore-mixture" for roasting. This is done by spreading out in thin layers, one upon the other, the different lots of ore, so that by cutting the mass down vertically, the charges taken daily for the furnace will have a pretty uniform composition. This is of great importance in its effect, both upon the roasting and also upon the regular working of the shaft furnace. The mixture contained in 1867:

60·645..................lead ores.
18·114..................."dry" or silver ores.
1·703..................copper ores.
11·779..................purchased products and flux.
7·759..................foreign ores.

100·

It contained on the average 0·2425 per cent. silver (70¾ oz.), 29·08 per cent. lead, and 0.156 per cent. copper.

Roasting:—The mixed ore, which is in the state of powder, is roasted in the reverberatory furnaces before mentioned. Experiment has proved that a hearth of 47 feet length, and a grate of 25 inches width, is sufficient to insure a thorough use of fuel with the above mixture of ores. The charge is made in posts of 1,650 pounds each, which are introduced every three hours, so that a furnace roasts 13,200 pounds in twenty-four hours. The thickness of the layer of ore is six inches. It should be remarked, however, that the new single hearth furnace, at the Halsbrücke works roasts 21,120 pounds daily. A great difference in the amount of labor is also apparent. The 76-foot, double hearth furnaces require eight workmen to twelve hours; the 47-foot furnaces, five men. Fuel amounts to 22½ per cent. of the ore, but the coal is of very poor quality and will average 20—25 per cent. of ash. Well roasted ore contains 3—5 per cent. sulphur, and rarely reaches 6 per cent. The ore is thoroughly fused and comes from the furnace as a silicate.

Reduction takes place in the octagonal or "Piltz" furnace, as it is named after its inventor. This was as first made octagonal, but new ones are to be round. The earlier forms were wider at the top than at the bottom, but the new ones are to have straight sides. The new furnaces then will differ from the old 7-tuyere Stolberg furnaces only in having one tuyere more, in having tuyeres on all sides, (and therefore, being cooled on all sides,) and in being closed at the top; their lower walls are only one brick thick, but this is a matter of convenience only and cannot have any material effect upon the working. Thinness of walls, in fact, has no other effect than to cool the hearth and thus prevent its rapid destruction.

The furnace is built in two parts. The upper part is built of any hard brick, is surrounded by a shell of strong sheet iron, and is carried upon eight iron columns. It stands 4½ feet above the sole of the hearth. Its shape being conical, and the base of the cone forming the top, the lining rests upon the iron shell, but the lower courses are also kept in place by a ring which is fastened to the shell by means of an angle iron.

The mode of supporting the shell upon the iron columns is somewhat peculiar. On four of the eight sides, a strip of angle iron is bolted to the shell. These rest upon an I beam bent to a square with rounded corners; and this I beam rests on the columns. The columns are not placed equi-distantly around the furnace, but are assembled in pairs on those sides where the angle iron is bolted on. At the level of the distributing air pipe brackets are placed on each side of the columns. Those on the outside carry the distributing pipe. Those next the furnace, bear against angle iron knuckles which are bolted to the shell, on those sides which do not carry the angle iron strips further up.

The top of the furnace is formed by a round iron hopper or cone, the opening of which is about 20 inches less than the diameter of the furnace. From this an iron cylinder projects into the furnace, leaving an open annular space of seven inches between the cylinder and the lining. The top of this cylinder is closed by a plain cylindrical sheet iron cup, resting on the inner surface of the hopper. The discharge flue is placed in the side immediately opposite the cylinder.

The charge is made in the hopper, around the cup, and is thrown into the furnace by raising the cup. It falls into the cylinder, and thence passes to the body of the furnace. The gas produced by the combustion of the fuel not being able to leave the furnace by the throat, collects in the annular space around the cylinder, and passes off by the flue. The flue is lined with firebrick, three inches thick.

This, as will be seen, is an old form of charging apparatus, well known to iron smelters. Other methods are also in use at Freiberg, in which the gas passes off by a central pipe, running through the cup. The reason for making the change was, that the system of flues is not sufficiently large for the work it has to do and the furnace sometimes failed to draw. The central pipe permits a direct discharge into the atmosphere whenever necessary.

The foundation is carried deep into the ground, and is surrounded by 2-inch plates of cast-iron. It consists, in fact, of an 8-sided iron box, lined with masonry. The center is filled up with slag, rubble, clay and bricks. Upon the masonry the hearth walls are built; and the hearth material, composed of clay and coke slack is laid on the bricks.

From this description, it will be seen, that the effective height of the furnace, that is, the height through which the products of combustion act on the charge, is that from the sole to the lower edge of the cylinder, or fifteen feet four inches.

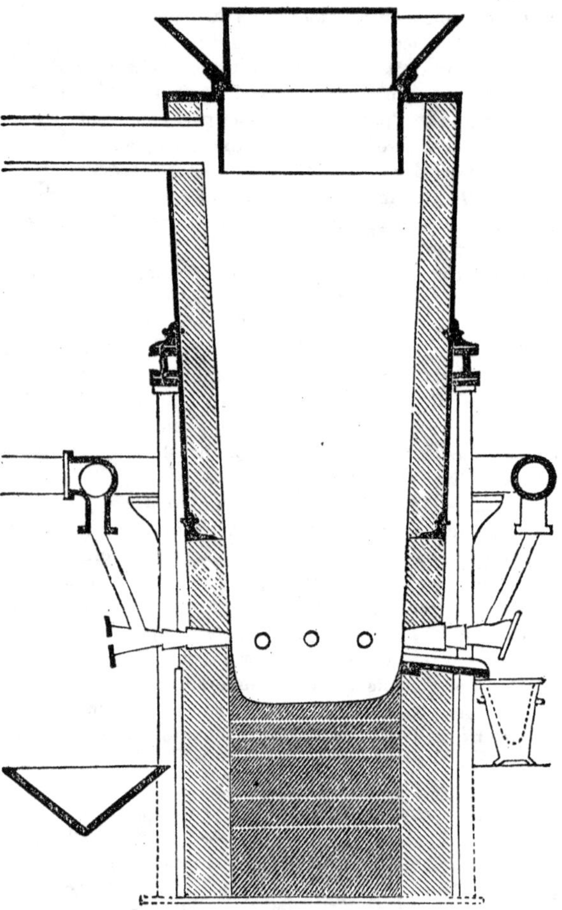

Figure 10.--Shaft Furnace at Freiberg. Vertical Section.

The dimensions of the furnace, reduced from French measure, are as follows:

Height from sole to top	17 feet 10 inches.
" of cylinder	2 " 6 "
" of slag discharge over sole	1 " 2 "
" of tuyeres over sole	1 " 9½ "
Diameter at tuyeres	5 " 1 "
" at top	6 " 5 "

Diameter of cylinder	5 feet 3 inches.
" of tuyeres	0 " 2½ "
Number of tuyeres (water cooled)	8
Hopper ; Height	1 ft. 9 in.
Diameter at top	8 " 9 "
" at bottom	4 " 8 "
Cup ; Height	2 " 4 "
Diameter	5 " 0 "
Blast pipes ; Diameter of distributing pipe (interior)	1 " 0 "
" of nozzle pipes	0 " 6 "
Discharge flue ; Diameter (interior)	1 " 3 "
Reception basin ; Diameter	4 " 0 "
Depth	1 " 5 "
Slag pot ; Height	2 " 1 "
Diameter at top	1 " 6 "
Columns ; Mean Diameter	6½ "
Height	14 " 2 "

The charge for the furnace is made up in layers like the ore-mixture, only not so carefully. Messrs. KAST and BRÄUNING give the following as its composition :

Roasted ore	100
Raw matte	15
Roasted pyrites from the kilns	15
Slag from the same operation	80—100
	210—230

But generally other products are worked into the charge such as arsenic residues, zinc residues, lead bearing products and purchased material, containing gold. Two furnaces (Stolberg) were in September, 1869, running on the following mixture of ores and products.

	I.	II.
Roasted ore	100	100
Slag from same operation	150	113.6
Raw matte	20	
Gold scraps	1·25	
Dezincing residue		10·9
	271·25	224·5

Freiberg ores contain gold, but in too small quantity to pay for extraction alone. But by increasing the proportion through the addition of gold scraps the whole is obtained. We have already seen that the material treated in 1869, contained as much as 106 pounds of this metal.

Products :—Lead, containing 0·5 per cent. (146 oz.) silver.

Matte, 0·2 per cent (58⅓ oz.) silver, 25 per cent. lead, and 6 per cent. copper.

Slag, 0·005 per—0·010 per cent. (0.6—1 oz.) silver, 5 lead.

Flue dust forms 1½ per cent. of the ore. It contains 0.005—0·01 per cent. silver, and 37—40 per cent. lead.

Of coke, containing 15—20 per cent. of ash, 10—11 per cent. is used. The pressure of blast is ¾—1 inch of mercury or ⅜—½ pound per square inch. One smelter, two chargers, and two to three slag-men are required to each shift.

Although the amount of silica in the charge is less than is considered advantageous in most lead works, no effort is made to increase it, but on the contrary basic fluxes—limestone and fluor spar are added. The result is a slag which is but little above a proto-silicate. The regulation of the charge depends upon the amount of zinc present. To avoid the formation of an infusible zinc slag, the proportion of sulphur is kept up, either by not roasting the ore completely or by adding raw ores or matte. This insures the passage of part of the zinc into the matte while another part unites with the slag. The amount of zinc present also

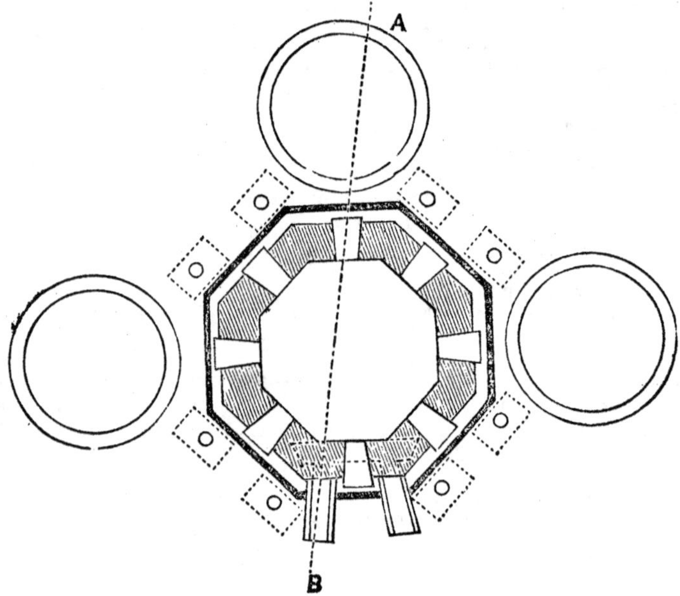

Figure 11.--Horizontal Section.

influences the proportion of slag repassed. At Halsbrücke, where the ores contain less zinc, the charge of slag from the same operation, is but one-half that used at the Mulden for zinciferous ores. This slag, according to Messrs. KAST and BRÄUNING, contains:

Silica	31·15	Barium Oxide	3·58
Iron oxide	41·31	Manganese oxide	2·10
Zinc oxide	7 85	Lead oxide	1·47
Alumina	3·18	Copper suboxide	0.16
Lime	6·45	Sulphur	1·85
Magnesia	1·06		
			100·17

The slag is received in conical iron pots. A certain amount of the lead and matte contained in it settles to the bottom and the points of the cones are broken off and sent at once to the next fusion. The amount of material treated in the lead process in 1867 was 18,359 tons, made up as follows:

9,071 tons lead ore.
3,330 " dry ore and copper ore.
5,303 " products containing iron (chiefly from the Preliminary Series of Operations.)
364 " arsenic residues.
270 " iron ore

THE TREATMENT OF THE MATTE.

The matte is roasted in kilns or stamped and roasted first in the Gerstenhöfer furnace, and when it is desired to reduce the amount of sulphur, in the reverberatory furnaces also. It is then smelted with the addition of slag from the first fusion.

The operation is in fact a treatment of the first slag with addition of the matte, and it exhibits in the strongest manner the peculiarities of the Freiberg methods. Though the matte is altogether basic, little acid flux is added; and even the slight amount of silica added, is swallowed up by the limestone and fluor spar which constantly form part of the charge. The aim is to produce a very basic, thin slag, which on account of its fluidity will allow the matte and lead to settle as perfectly as possible.

The charge varies very much, for this fusion is the general outlet of whatever the works afford of basic products. Messrs. KAST & BRAUNING give the following as a specimen: They, it will be observed, base the charge upon the amount of first slag it contains. This view is certainly correct, as this slag forms by far the largest part of the charge, and the operation is really a refusion of slag.

Slag from first fusion	100·0	Speise	1·0
Copper slag	4·0	Dezincing Residues	1 0
Copper matte raw	2 3	Limestone	2·0
Lead matte roasted in kilns	4.3	Fluor spar	2·0
Lead matte roasted in kilns and stalls	8·4	Hearth, etc	7·2
Pyrites	9·0		
			141·2

Thus, matte and ore form but 26 parts to 100 slag. On September 16, 1869, the charge was:

First slag	100
Roasted first matte	20
Fluor spar	10
Copper slag	5
	134

Labor and pressure of blast are the same as before. Of fuel 13–14 per cent. is consumed, equal to 17—18 per cent. of the slag; or 70—75 per cent. of the matte and ore.

Products:—Lead=0.15–0·18 per cent. (44—52 oz.) silver.
2nd matte—0·10—0 20 per cent. silver, 21 per cent. lead, and 15 per cent. copper.
2nd slag=0·002 per cent. (½ oz.) silver, 1·5—2 per cent. lead. This slag is thrown away.

There are no full analyses of the slag, but the proportion of some of its constituents is as follows:

Silica	29·7
Zinc oxide	8·5

Lead oxide .... 2·5
Silver.. 0·0025

The extremely basic character of this slag, and its large percentage of zinc, make the management of the furnace very difficult. When the Piltz furnace was first introduced at the Muldner works, its height was made 22 feet; but its reducing action was too great for the slag, and it had to be cut down. A new furnace which is to be built will be eleven feet eight inches high, the diameter of five feet one inche being retained. Its sides wi l be straight instead of inclined.

Third and Fourth Fusions:—The second matte is twice roasted and resmelted with first slag, the object being to concentrate it to about 23 per cent. copper, when it is looked upon as a copper matte. These fusions form successive steps in the operation last described. The working of the fu nace is not stopped, but a second or third matte is merely substituted for the first, for a few days or until the whole of the material at hand has been smelted. The other constituents of the charge remain the same, and the expense of labor and fuel is not to be distinguished from that given for the second fusion An old table, showing the gradual change of the matte from a lead matte carrying about 57 ounces of silver to the ton, to a copper matte with one-third less silver is given below; but it is very likely that the new method has changed these proportions.

	SILVER. Decreases.		LEAD. Decreases.	COPPER. Increases.
	Per cent.	Oz. in 2000 lbs.	Per cent.	Per cent.
1st matte	0.25	73	25	6
2nd do	0·23	66 24	21	15
3d do	0·17	48·96	13	32
4th do	0·15	43·75	13	42

In the processes just described, the ores have all been treated and resolved first into the side products obtained in the preliminary series of operations; and into two others—lead and copper matte—the result of the shaft furnac treatment. In the lead is concentrated nearly all the gold and silver, and the remaining operations of the regular series are those belonging to the lead treatment, by which the gold and silver are separated from the former metal; and those belonging to the copper process, in which copper, vitriol, and rich silver residues are obtained.

TREATMENT OF THE LEAD.

The lead obtained in the foregoing operations contains a very appreciable amount of iron, copper, arsenic, and antimony. It is all refined by heating in a reverberatory furnace, with admission of air. The above metals are all more oxidizable than lead, and a product is obtained in which they are concentrated. This is used to make hard lead, while the refined metal goes through the Pattison process, for the extraction of its silver. The latter process has been so often described, that it will not be followed here. Fourteen kettles are in use, each of 27,500 pounds capacity; concentration proceeds on the one-third system, and poor lead is obtained with 0·0015 per cent. silver, and rich lead of 1·5 per cent.—1.8 per cent. (437—505 oz.) silver. The consumption of fuel in twenty-four hours is 4,220 pounds.

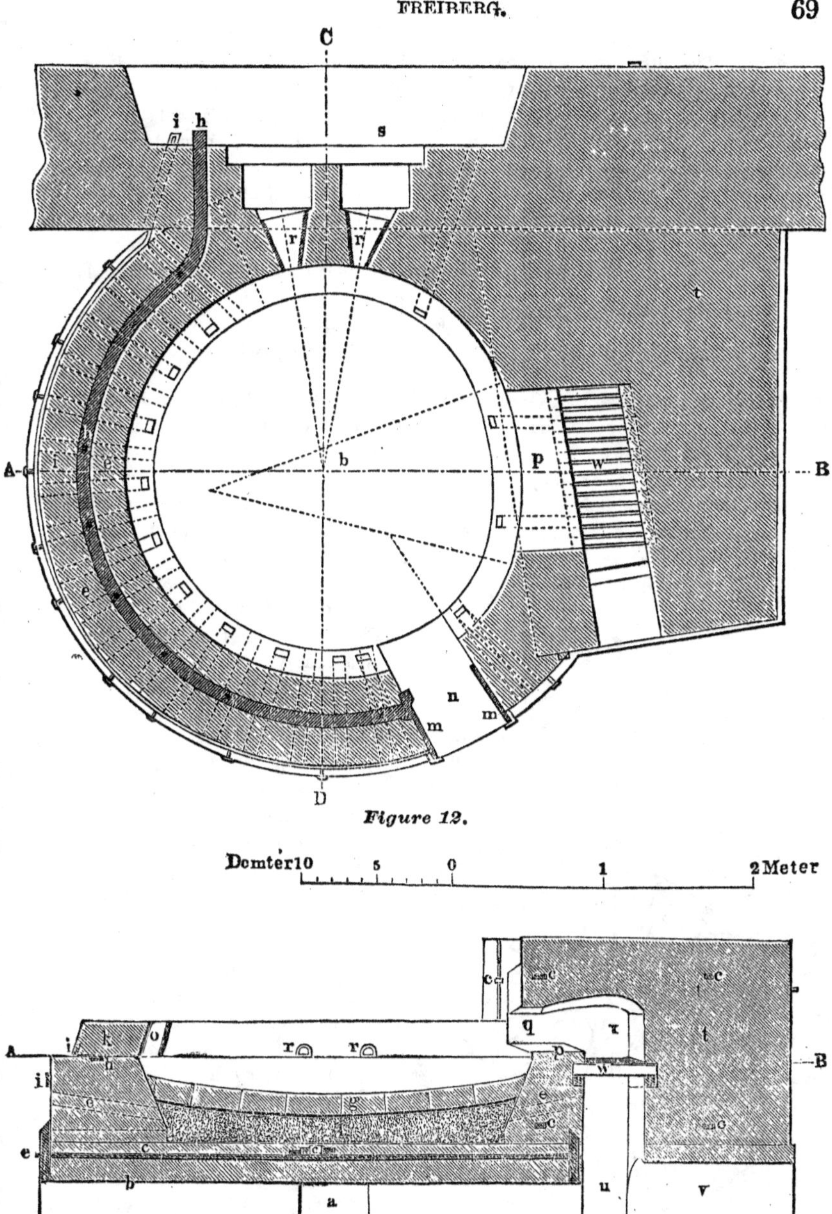

Figure 12.

Figure 13.

Refining:—Two furnaces are in use, one shallow and one deep, the dimensions having a marked effect upon the consumption of fuel.

The shallow furnace treats 10 tons in 24 hours, with 2,200 pounds coal.

The deep " " 13·6—16 tons " " 1,320—1760 pounds coal.

In spite of this extreme difference in fuel, the saving by the deep furnace is, at Freiberg, but a few cents to a ton of lead; the coal being very cheap.

Products:—Lead, containing 0·6 per cent. (175 oz.) silver.

1st. Abstrich, which amounts to about 19 per cent. of the charge. It contains a great deal of lead arsenate and antimonate, and a little copper and iron sulphide.

2nd. Abstrich, forming 10 per cent. of the charge, and containing but little arsenic or antimony. This is returned to the first fusion for lead.

Cupellation is performed in a German hearth. It is divided into three stages, forming three separate operations. 1. The operation is stopped at the point at which the bismuth begins to oxidise. This takes place when the lead is so concentrated as to contain about 50 per cent. silver. 2. The rich lead is then removed to a new furnace and concentrated to about 85—90 per cent. silver. All the products contain bismuth and are treated for this metal. 3. Refining takes place at the Halsbrücke works, the products being also rich in bismuth.

Figure 14.

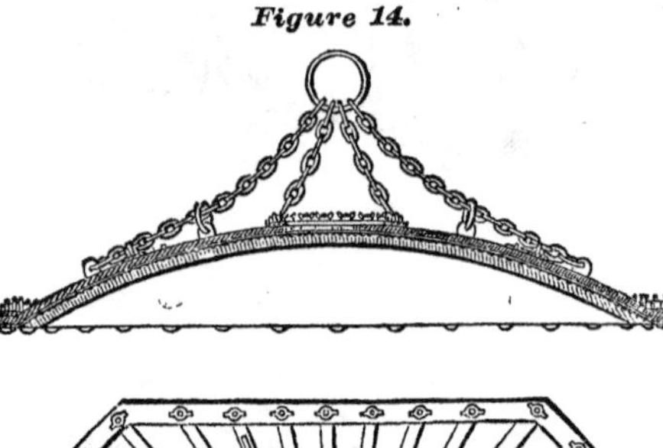

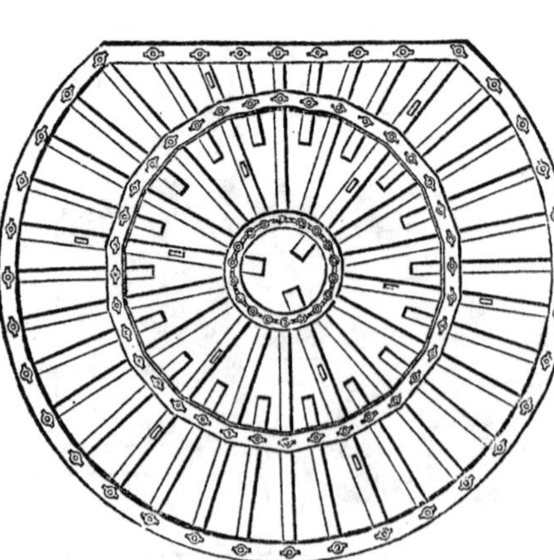

Figure 15.

The operation is performed in a cupel furnace, shown in Figures 12, 13, 14, and 15. This is a round furnace, with concave, or cup-shaped hearth, the arch of which is formed of sheet iron lined with clay and removable. The lead is charged in the hearth with the cover removed, and when ready the cover is placed by means of a crane and the joint luted with clay. There are five openings to the hearth, one for the flames to enter, two for the blast, one by which the abzug is drawn out and one for the discharge of the litharge. Figure 12 is a view of the hearth with the cover removed, dotted lines showing the relative angles of the blast, flame and litharge openings. Figure 13 is vertical section, also without the cover, and Fig. 14 and 15 show the skeleton of the cover;

b is the foundation wall, *c* the iron braces, *d* drying canals, *e* ring wall, often made of clay, packed within an outer ring of masonry, *f* sole, of slag from lead furnace, *g* brick sole laid on the slag. This is laid dry and the crevices calked with mergel. Upon this is stamped a mergel sole (not shown in the figure) which forms the working sole of the furnace. Mergel is an argillaceous limestone stamped fine and when of good quality, contains about 22 silica, 6 clay, 4 iron, 2 magnesia and 66 lime carbonate. When no natural rock of about this composition is at hand artificial mergel may be made by mixing intimately 1 volume clay with 3 to 4 volumes powdered limestone. The powder is sifted through a mesh of 64 holes to the square inch. This is mixed with old hearth powdered, moistened and stamped in upon the brick sole, the layer being 2 – 3 inches thick. In stamping the mass may be placed in layers, the face of each layer being criss-crossed before putting in the next, or the whole may be put in at once, lightly stamped to shape, and finished by stamping in a spiral line from the wall to the center. In the center, sometimes nearer the firebridge, a shallow basin is cut out where the silver finally collects. When finished the sole must be so hard that pressure with the fingers makes no impression upon it. The object of the sole is to absorb the litharge formed in the last stages of the operation It must, therefore, be porous, but not so porous as to absorb too much litharge. The shape of the sole has some effect upon the operation. An old rule is that with a deep hearth the lead oxidizes easier, but the silver brightens less easily ; with a shallow hearth the brightening is easier, the formation of litharge slower.

In the figures *h* and *i* are iron ring braces, *k* brick wall forming the sides of the hearth, *m* iron plate covered with mergel, forming the litharge opening *n* ; this usually has a hood to draw off lead fumes and protect the workmen ; *o* opening where the flames escape and the abzug is drawn off; this furnace has no chim ey but is placed under a large chimney forming the cupellation room ; *p* fire bridge *r* tuyeres, *u* and *v* ash pit, *w* grate.

The cover is made of iron bars joined by concentric iron rings upon which are placed segments of sheet iron. The sheet iron is pierced with numerous holes through which project bent pieces of hoop iron. Upon this a tough clay mixed with sand is thrown, forming the interior surface of the hood. These different parts are shown in Figure 15.

Of the cupellation a good idea will be obtained from five operations, in 1869, which gave the following results :

Charge :	Lead from Pattinsoning	286,165	pounds.
Products :	Abzug	1,100	"
	Abstrich	none.	
	Red litharge	30,910	"
	Bismuth litharge	4,290	"
	Ordinary litharge	221,760	"
	Lead scraps	3,410	"
	Hearth	25,080	"

The working time was 463 hours, but this evidently does not include the time employed in preparing and drying the furnace. The average amount of lead cupelled was 552 pounds per hour ; a very high figure, and due to the fact that towards 30 tons of lead are cupelled at each operation. Of fuel 4¼ cords wood,

15,400 pounds brown coal, and 6,610 pounds bituminous coal were used; or per ton of lead, 0·03 cords wood, 108 pounds brown coal, and 46 pounds coal (7·7 per cent.)

Of the above products the red litharge is sold for paint; the litharge containing bismuth is treated for that metal; ordinary litharge is revived to lead, lead scraps are returned to the next cupellation, and the hearth is charged in the first fusion for lead.

Second Cupellation:—The rich lead is not weighed but usually from 1,300 to 1,800 pounds weight, are obtained at each operation. From this second cupellation, which is conducted like the first, the following products are obtained:

First litharge, containing 4 per cent. bismuth.

Second litharge containing 9—10 per cent. bismuth.

Hearth containing 9—10 per cent. bismuth.

The time is four to six hours, fuel 9,380 pounds coal.

The resulting silver is refined in a cupel furnace. It contains all the gold of the ores and products, and this is separated by the usual method of dissolving the silver in hot sulphuric acid. The gold remains as a residue, and the silver is precipitated by copper from the solution. The gold is ignited with saltpeter and melted with bisulphate of soda. The slag contains platinum, which is obtained from it in the chemical laboratory.

THE COPPER PROCESS.[2]

Hitherto we have followed the course of the operations as they are carried out at the Muldner works; now we will turn our attention to the Halsbrücke works where all the copper is extracted. The matte is subjected to one more operation, by which its percentage of copper is increased to 73—75 per cent. This is done by a peculiar process.

The first copper matte, according to analysis made in the Clausthal laboratory (and the specimen may be looked upon as a fair average, though the copper sometimes rises to 43 per cent.), is made up as follows:—

Copper	32·9	Iron	19·5
Silver	0·25	Sulphur	23·8
Lead	15.		

Arsenic, antimony, zinc, nickel, cobalt, etc., in small quantities.

This is smelted in a reverberatory furnace with quartz and barium sulphate. By reduction the barium sulphate becomes barium sulphide, which, in presence of copper oxide, gives up its sulphur to the copper, takes oxygen, and forms a silicate with the quartz. This use of barium sulphate as a re-agent is intended to prevent the introduction of iron into the charge. Since metallic copper is not made, but copper sulphate instead, it is necessary to the purity of the latter that the resulting matte shall not contain more than 0·2 per cent. of iron. The matte is stamped and roasted in a reverberatory furnace, to 5 per cent. sulphur. This is over-roasting, for there is not enough sulphur left to make the basic copper sulphide which is desired. But over-roasting is necessary in order to oxidize the

2 This account of the treatment of the copper products is taken from that by Professor Kuhlemann of the Clausthal School of Mines, in the Preuss. Zeitschrift für Berg, Hütten und Salinen Wesen, 1872.

iron sufficiently to insure its removal. Sulphur is then added to the charge in the form, as above stated, of barium sulphate, and by this method copper matte, of a high degree of concentration, and of a purity that is hardly attempted elsewhere than at Freiberg, is obtained.

In roasting, the charge is 1,100—1,540 pounds of matte every three hours ; or 8,800—11,320 pounds in twenty-four hours. The furnace is kept cooler than with ores or other matte, because the copper matte is very liable to soften and sinter. Of coal 30—36 per cent. is used, but it is of very poor quality, containing 20—25 per cent. of ash.

The product contains copper oxide, basic copper sulphate, iron oxide, basic iron sulphate, metallic silver, silver oxide, lead sulphate, zinc oxide, nickel oxide, cobalt oxide, and arsenic and antimony salts.

This is fused in a reverberatory of the kind described when speaking of the preparatory operations. The sides, formed of clay and quartz sand, are repaired after every two or three operations, because the slag, being a singulo silicate, attacks them rapidly. The charge weighs 3,630—3,960 pounds. Immediately after charging the furnace is fired as hotly as possible for 4—5 hours, when the charge is stirred, and when the matte has settled, the scoria is raked off, the matte remaining behind. A second charge is immediately made, and when the scoria from that has been drawn off, a third. Not until the matte of three charges has collected is it tapped. Five charges are made in twenty-four hours. The following is the composition of a charge :—

Charge :—		
	Roasted matte	100
	Raw copper (from same operation)	14—27
	Black copper (from same operation)	23
	Barium sulphate	25—30
	Raw quartzose dry ores	14—23

Sometimes fluor spar is added to make the slag more fusible.

Products :—Black copper, containing lead, 0·50—0·60 per cent. silver, 20—25 lead, 50—60 per cent. copper.

Concentrated matte : 0·29—0·40 per cent silver, 3—7 per cent. lead, 70—73 per cent. copper. This product is the one for which the operation is undertaken

Copper matte : 0·30—0·40 per cent. silver, 9 per cent. lead, 60 per cent. copper.

Of these products the black copper and copper matte are returned raw to the same operation.

There was an *apparent* loss of 0·26 per cent. silver, and 0·05 per cent. copper, and an apparent gain of 21·85 per cent. lead, and 296·35 per cent. gold. This arises from the fact that both the dry ores and scoria contained lead and silver which was in too small quantity to be accounted for by the assayer, as in keeping the books of the establishment each process is charged and credited with the materials it receives and delivers on the same principles which govern the purchase of ores. The figures of loss and profit are, therefore, not real, but financial.

The resulting concentrated matte contained, by analysis :

Copper	76·4	Iron	0·14
Lead	4·2	Sulphur	14·05—95·08
Silver	0·29		

In this specimen the percentage of copper is somewhat above the average. An average matte contains 69—74 per cent. copper, 0·2 per cent. nickel and cobalt. and 0.5—1 per cent. arsenic and antimony.

This matte is now treated with hot sulphuric acid to extract the copper. It is first stamped dry and sifted through a mesh of about 32 to the square inch in order to separate the metallic copper always existing in a matte of so high a grade. This metallic co per, if allowed to remain, would pass through the dissolving process almost undissolved, since the time of that operation is calculated for the solution of copper oxide, which is much quicker than that of the metal. The powdered matte is then roasted dead in an Augustin muffle furnace that has three hearths, and is so arranged that the hot gases can be shut off wholly or partly from the middle hearth, the object being to protect the fresh charge from the action of the hot gases. If too hot, the matte might soften sufficiently to sinter. One charge only of 1,000 pounds is at one time in the furnace, which for six hours is kept quite dark, the heat being then increased for three hours to incipient whiteness, which is kept up for three hours more under constant stirring of the matte. The charge remains sixteen hours in the furnaces, and its sulphur is reduced to 1 per cent. The roasted ore should be bluish black from copper oxide and not reddish brown which would indicate iron oxide. Labor amounts to about six days to 2,000 pounds, and of coal, which must be of the best quality, 110—120 per cent. is consumed.

The roasted matte is sifted to remove the lumps formed in roasting. These enclose raw particles which would pass unchanged through the dissolving process and add to the amount of the argentiferous residues. These coarse particles are stamped and re-roasted ; the fine part is ground in mills and bolted. It consists of oxides of copper, iron, nickel, cobalt and lead, metallic copper, silver and gold ; a small quantity of sulphates of copper and lead ; and some arsenic and antimony salts.

When this is boiled with sulphuric acid the oxides are dissolved, but metallic copper, silver and gold mostly remain as a residue. If silver is dissolved it is re-precipitated by the copper present. Arsenic and antimony salts are broken up, the arsenic remaining in the liquor as free arsenious acid, and the antimony as antimonic hydrate which partly falls.

The solution of the oxides takes place in thick vats of hard lead, having a capacity of 1.25 cubic meters, or about 45 cubic feet. They are 1.1 meter high and 1.22—1·36 meters in diameter Raw chamber acid of 49—50° B. is first introduced to the height of 0.36 meters, and super heated steam is blown in until the liquor boils. This dilutes it somewhat. The powdered matte is gradually added by means of percussion troughs, during which the whole is stirred constantly. One of the drawbacks of the Freiberg method is the tendency of the matte to lump together, thus increasing the amount of residue. Boiling is continued for an hour and a half, when the vat is filled up with mother liquor from the crystallization tanks, and the boiling continued. The solution then marks 32° B. It is allowed to settle for two hours, and the clear liquor is then drawn off by a syphon to the clarifying vats, and afterwards to the crystallization tanks. The entire operation lasts five hours, and with four dissolving vats 3,630 pounds of matte are treated in twenty-four hours.

Crystallization continues for nine days. The first vitriol formed—about one quarter of the whole—goes to the market as raw vitriol. The remaining three quarters is re-dissolved, filtered through granulated copper to remove the insoluble residue, and also precipitate any silver that may be in solution, and recrystallized. This operation also takes nine days. The new liquor is nearly neutral, and the crystals are very large; they are washed to remove a brown coating, and dried.

The yearly production is about 2,300,000 pounds, from 880,000 pounds of matte. The number of vats is eight, and of crystallization tanks 104.

The mother liquor is concentrated by boiling, and a new crop of crystals taken. These contain 0.035 per cent of iron. The mother liquor is now very rich in iron, but it also contains two pounds of copper to the cubic foot. It is used as a cementing liquor in making fine pyritiferous ore into bricks. By this means the copper is returned to the process.

The Residues contain the silver. They are washed, filtered and dried, and form about 17 per cent. of the concentrated matte. Their composition in 1869 was about 1.94 per cent. silver, 41 per cent. lead and 11 per cent. copper; but the proportion of copper has since then been reduced to 5 per cent. by using stronger acid. The percentage of lead is large, because the sulphate of this metal is entirely insoluble, and lead sulphate is formed by the action of the sulphuric acid. These residues are added to the first fusion for lead.

The balance sheet, reckoned upon 100 parts by weight of concentrated matte, is as follows:

Charge:—Concentrated matte		100
Sheet copper		22—122
Raw chamber acid reduced to 66° B (by weight)		196·7—196·7
Products:—Copper sulphate		251 38
Residues		16·41
Mother liquor=3 pounds copper per cubic foot		68 cubic feet
Do. do. ferruginous, for bricks, 2lbs copper per cubic foot		180 "
Labor:—Roasting, days of twenty-four hours,	16	
Extraction, "	7·55—23·55	
Fuel:—Roasting	116·6	
Heating boiler	124·5	
" liquor	100·8	
Drying crystals	20·0	
" residues	6·3—368·2	

If to the above 251·38 cwt. of copper sulphate from 100 cwt. of concentrated matte we add the 8 cwt., to be extracted from the 68 cubic feet of 3-pound mother liquor, we have a total of 259·38 cwt. of copper sulphate from 71·5 cwt.

of copper in the matte. The make is, therefore, 362·8 per cent., and 100 parts of copper require 176·1 parts of acid of 66° B, to make 362·8 parts of copper sulphate. This proportion of acid is 21·5 parts in excess of that demanded by chemical laws, an excess which is accounted for by the acid taken up by the lead oxide.

It should be remembered that the coal used contains for the most part 20—30 per cent. of ash; the remainder holding 8—10 per cent. All of it has about 8 per cent. of water.

The loss amounted to 3·10 per cent. gold, 0·65 per cent silver, and 0·64 per cent. copper. The gain was 20·48 per cent. lead, these amounts, as before said, not representing real loss or gain, but the commercial values of the materials treated and the products obtained.

SUPPLEMENTARY SERIES.

Among those operations which, in the early part of this paper, were referred to as merely supplementary to the regular course of the process are the Treatment of the Hard Lead; Manufacture of Arsenic; Extraction of Bismuth; Separation of Gold and Extraction of Platinum.

The material treated in these operations consists of: 1. First abstrich from the refining of the lead; 2. Crude arsenic from the arsenic ores; 3. Litharge and hearth, containing bismuth, from the cupellation; and 4. The alloy of gold, silver and platinum obtained in cupellation.

Desilverization of the abstrich:—The abstrich, which forms about 19 per cent. of the lead obtained from the blast furnaces, contains 5—6 per cent. antimony, 6—7 per cent. arsenic, and 0·2 per cent. copper. It is mixed with 3—4 per cent. coal, and heated in a reverberatory furnace. By this method a small quantity of the abstrich is reduced to lead, which is much richer in silver than the part of the abstrich which remains unreduced. The products are:

Lead, which goes to the lead treatment.

Desilvered abstrich=0·001 per cent. silver, 8 per cent. antimony, 7 per cent. arsenic, and 0·17 per cent. copper; to treatment of hard lead.

Fusion for hard lead:—This desilvered abstrich is charged in a shaft furnace, the charge being as follows:

Charge:—100 Desilvered abstrich.
25 Slag from fusion for lead.
5 Fluor spar.

Products:

Hard lead=0·01 per cent. silver, 9—14 per cent. antimony, 3 per cent. arsenic, and 0·4 per cent. copper. To refining.

Abstrich scoria=15 per cent. lead.

Treatment of abstrich scoria:—It is fused again with 25 per cent. slag from the fusion for lead, and 5 per cent. fluor spar. The products are hard lead, which is added to that obtained in the last operation; and 2d, abstrich scoria, which is sent to the fusion of matte.

Refining of Hard Lead:—The hard lead obtained in the last two fusions is refined in a reverberatory. Arsenic and copper are more easily oxidized than lead and antimony, and two products are obtained, one rich in the former, and the other in the latter metals. These products are :

1. Refined hard lead=9—14 per cent. antimony, 2 per cent. arsenic, 0·15 per cent. copper. To poling.
2. Scraps=12 per cent. antimony, 4 per cent. arsenic, and 9 per cent. copper. This is reduced to metal by fusion with 25 per cent. lead scoria, and 5 per cent. fluor, in a shaft furnace.

Poling of Hard Lead:—This operation, by which the amount of arsenic is still further reduced, consists of plunging green wood into the melted lead contained in a Pattinson kettle. The result is :

1. Lead scraps.
2. Marketable Hard lead=9—15 per cent. antimony, 1·2—1·8 per cent. arsenic, 0·15 per cent. copper.

The object of these repeated operations is to separate the arsenic and obtain a lead, the hardness of which shall be due mainly to antimony, as this is the constituent which makes this impure lead valuable.

Manufacture of Arsenic. Refining:—The production of commercial arsenic from arsenical residues of the sulphuric acid process, and from flue dust, was mentioned in treating of the preliminary operations, for the reason that these products are mixed with the ores of the metal, and the two classes of operations are inseparable. Therefore to that description remains to be added only the process of refining, It is only the arsenic made from ores that requires refining, the product obtained from the flue dust being already sufficiently pure. The former is refined by redistillation in closed kettles. These kettles must be made of an iron containing as little carbon as possible, since the carbon will darken the glass by reducing a part of the arsenious acid to a lower degree of oxidation. The kettles serve for 150 charges, though made very thin. There are two setts, each containing 5 kettles; the labor amounts to 1 man to each sett. Yellow arsenic is made from white by adding a small quantity of sulphur. The intensity of color depends upon the proportion of sulphur, and the quantity of the latter is usually 2 per cent.

The Extraction of Bismuth:—Only a very small part of the ore contains bismuth in sufficient quantity to warrant any payment for the metal. But minute quantities, so small as to escape the assayer, or, at all events, too small to be worth reckoning in the price, are found in much of the ore. The bismuth is reduced like the lead, and follows that metal in all the manipulations up to cupellation. It is, however, more difficult to oxidize than lead, but less so than silver. The first portions of lead oxidized in the cupel furnace, therefore, contain no bismuth, but when the lead is enriched to about 50 per cent. silver, the bismuth also begins to oxidize, and is found in the litharge and hearth.

These products are placed in large earthen jars, of 10 cubic feet capacity, and treated with diluted hydrochloric acid, the proportions being 100 lbs. litharge and hearth to 120 lbs. acid. The acid remains 5--6 hours, or until the heat arising from the chemical action subsides. The jar is then filled up with cold water and the contents well stirred, after which they are suffered to rest for 12 hours and the clear liquid is then drawn off by means of a syphon, into a tank holding 50 cubic feet. This tank is filled up with cold water, which throws down basic bismuth chloride hydrate.

The residues are treated 9 or 10 times with quantities of acid decreasing from 20 to 5 lbs., and the liquor is as before drawn off into the large tank.

The basic bismuth chloride is fused in iron crucibles with soda carbonate, coal and quartz. In 1868 the production of bismuth was about 44,000 lbs., worth nearly $3 25 a pound. The direct cost of manufacture was only 65 cents a pound, not counting in the extra amount of cupel hearth, which is produced by dividing the cupellation into two operations.

The separation of gold and platinum was included in the treatment of the silver. These operations do not differ from the ordinary methods, and hardly come within the province of this paper, which is intended to exhibit Freiberg as a lead and copper producing establishment.

In reviewing the processes in use at Freiberg, it is evident that with all their excellences, some of them have great defects. Many of the lesser operations evince an amount of skill and of scientific ingenuity which is rarely met with. But on the other hand, the most important of all the operations—the fusion for lead—is carried on in a way not to be commended. One of the chief purposes of a fusion of ores is, in nearly all cases, to dispose once and for all of that portion of the ore which is of no value—the gangue. It is of importance to get out as much metal at one fusion as possible, but it is of at least equal importance to produce in the first operation a slag which is sufficiently poor to be thrown away. This is not done at Freiberg. The products from the fusion of lead ore all require re-smelting. That is inevitable with the lead and the matte, for by the nature of the case both have valuable constituents, which must be separated. But the slag is re-smelted only because it has about 5 per cent. of lead, and slags are not usually considered worthless until their proportion of lead has been reduced to 1½ per cent., or less. If we assume these products to be in the proportion of 28 lead, 25 matte, and 47 slag, we see that fully one-third of the ore ought to leave the treatment once for all at this step; it should be thrown away as useless slag. The fact that it is not thrown away entails considerable expense of fuel and labor. If it were possible to reject at once 33 of the 47 per cent. of slag, the saving in fuel alone would amount to at least 3 per cent. of the original ore.

The fault of the operation is the formation of a basic slag. To this is due the retention of so much lead. Basic slags are, as a rule, avoided in lead smelting, the slag from lead works in all quarters of the world having, with tolerable uniformity, pretty nearly the composition of a bisilicate. The composition of worthless lead slags may, as a rule, be put at 35—40 per cent. silica. and over 40 per cent. iron oxide, the remainder being bases of various kinds. In many works the amount of zinc closely approaches that in the Freiberg slag. These facts indicate that to place the lead treatment at Freiberg on a par with that of other works, it is necessary to increase the proportion of silica in the charge without lowering that of iron oxide ; that is, the slag must be raised from a proto-silicate (nearly), as at present, to one that is nearly a bi-silicate. The problem is then, Is there any means of doing this? Difficult as it is to prescribe means of working in an establishment so distant as the great Saxon works, and daring as is the task of criticizing the management of men so able and so experienced as those who control it, it still seems to me possible to indicate a theoretical method of reforming this process. Whether that reformation is practicable is a question of dollars and cents, which only the most intimate acquaintance with the special conditions of Freiberg can determine.

The Freiberg mines are situated in the midst of a great field of gneiss, of which three kinds are distinguished. The composition of these is given by SCHEERER as follows:

	I.	II.	III.	Mean.
Silica	65·26	70·75	75·24	70·45
Titanic acid	0·95	0·50	0·20	0·55
Clay	14·82	13·70	12·86	13 79
Iron oxide } Manganese oxide }	6·20	5·17	2·34	4·57
Lime	2·98	2·08	0 95	2·00
Magnesia	1·88	1·07	0·36	1·10
Potassa	3·93	3 34	4·86	4 04
Soda	2·43	2·42	2·30	2·38
Water	1·06	1 03	0·68	0·92
	99·60	100 06	99·80	99·80

Here, then, we have a substance capable of supplying the needed silica. But if this alone were added to the charge, the amount of iron would be decreased, and the average given by KAST and BRÄUNING for the Muldner slag (40 per cent. iron oxide) is already as low as it ought to be. Iron must be added in some form, and probably the cheapest supply could be obtained at the iron works in the neighborhood of Freiberg. Both puddle and reheating slag can be had and in quantity sufficient to satisfy the demands even of works that treat 25,000—30,000 tons of ore a year. This material can be had by paying the expense of removal, which, from Camsdorf, would be, delivered at Freiberg, about $1 a ton. There are other works nearer Freiberg, from which the same slag could probably be obtained at less cost.

At present a large amount of slag from the same operation is smelted with the ore. It yields nothing, for it leaves the furnace with just as much lead as it had when it entered. But it makes the fusion easier, and also regulates the run by diluting any impurity in the ore—as an exceptional amount of zinc oxide. If this charge of slag were entirely or partially replaced by a proper amount of the gneiss and the iron slag, the composition of the charge could be regulated at will and without increasing the amount of material treated. Let us see what the proper proportion would be.

The mean composition of the reheating and puddle slag may be taken, in the absence of analyses, at 60 iron oxide and 40 silica. Assuming that it is desired to make a lead slag containing 38 silica and 45 iron oxide, the amount of the two fluxes necessary to transform 100 parts of the present Muldner slag into a slag of the new composition is the following:

	Muldner slag. 100 parts.	Gneiss. 20 parts.	Iron slag. 85 parts.	Total.
Silica	31	14	34	79
Iron oxide	41	1	51	93
Other bases	28	5		33
				205

These melted together would give a slag containing, in round numbers, silica 38·5, iron oxide 45·3 and other bases 16·2 per cent. According to KAST and BRÄUNING, 100 parts of ore and matte in the lead process yield about 25 lead and 23 matte. The slag must therefore amount to about 50 per cent. of the ore and matte in the charge. Calculating the amount of the proposed fluxes to be added to 100 parts of lead ore, roasted pyrites and matte, as usually charged at the Muldner works, we have the following quantities required:

	New charge.	Old charge.
Muldner ore, etc	100	100
Gneiss	10	
Reheat. and pud. slag	43	
Slag from same operation	10	60--75

In this estimate, which is not meant to be exact, no account has been taken of the basic fluxes—limestone and fluor spar—now added to the charge, and which, of course, would be useless in the new charge. The removal of these would decrease to some extent the amount of gneiss required.

It is well known that the fusion of raw fluxes costs more fuel and requires a higher temperature than that of fluxes which have already been melted. But in the proposed charge the amount of gneiss is too small (7 per cent. of the whole charge, or less) to alter the present conditions of the furnace materially. It is quite probable, in fact, that the reduction of the zinc oxide in the slag by one-third, and the production of a more fusible slag, would fully neutralize the disadvantage of smelting down the small quantity of raw flux required.

One of the greatest difficulties met with at Freiberg is the amount of zinc present in the charge. Care has to be taken to manage the previous roasting, and the composition of the shaft furnace charge, so that only a part of the zinc shall pass into the slag and part into the matte. When the amount of zinc oxide is right the old slag repassed has no effect upon it, for it contains just as much of the zinc oxide as the charge has. But the addition of fresh material would be of great advantage, for it would take up its share of the zinc and thus lower the percentage in the whole amount of slag. If the slag from 100 ore, without gneiss and iron slag, contains 10 per cent. of zinc oxide, that made from the same ore, with an addition of 53 parts of those fluxes, would contain only about 6·5 per cent.

A slag of this kind, formed according to the principles which have been proved in numberless works, and containing a not excessive amount of zinc, ought to be sufficiently poor in lead to be at once thrown away. In proof of this, and as an indication of what results spring from comparatively slight changes in the composition of slags, I will cite again the analyses of the lead slag from the first matte fusion, as it is thrown away, at the Muldner and Halsbrücke works:

	Muldner.	Halsbrücke.
Silica	29·7	34.1
Zinc oxide	8 5	7·6
Lead oxide	2·5	1·0
Silver	0 0025	0·0015
Lead oxide in previous ore slag	5·7	1·37

The Halsbrücke slag, it will be observed, has about the composition of the ideal slag proposed above.

The Freiberg metallurgists may have some occult reason for smelting their ore twice over. It is not to be supposed that with such excellent materials for flux about them they have considered themselves forced to the course they have taken. But what those reasons are no traveller has yet discovered. The Freiberg works are a splendid example of the success with which the products of a large mining district may be treated in one or two works; and the explanation of the faulty lead process has usually been sought for in the diversity and difficulty of the ores subjected to it. That, however, as before remarked, cannot be the case, and it is to be hoped that among the valuable treatises on metallurgy which occasionally come from the great mining town of Saxony, there will some day be one which will let the outer world into the secret of the present system. At present Freiberg may fairly be said to be pursuing one path and the rest of the world another. The reasons for a course so singular must lie either in general principles or in special conditions of the place; if the former, it might aid the cause of mining in the world to know what these principles are.

The Lead and Silver Works of the Hartz Mountains.

The mining region of the Hartz mountains* is second in importance to that of Saxony alone. Indeed, if the Mansfield copper mines are added to the silver, lead and copper mines of the Upper Hartz we have a district which is in every respect —extent, value of product, number of workmen and intelligent methods of work— the equal of any other similar region in the world. The subject of the present paper is the smelting operations at Clausthal, Lautenthal and Altenau. In former times the "Upper Hartz" was a name given to the works at Clausthal, Lautenthal, Altenau and Andreasberg, each of which had a completely furnished smelting establishment where argentiferous lead ores could be resolved into merchantable lead, silver and copper. When the district passed into the hands of the Prussians in consequence of the war of 1866, changes were made which placed the region very much higher than it had ever been in the scale of importance. The mines

* Changes have followed each other so rapidly in the Hartz that almost every year has brought out some new process or important modification of old methods. The above notes, therefore, though based on personal observation, have been mainly drawn from the writings of Koch, Wedding and Bræuning and Kuhlemann. With the exception of Dr. Wedding all of these gentlemen are actively engaged in the works they have described.

were worked more vigorously, and plans were laid out for increasing the amount of ore treated to 400,000 centners or 20,000 tons (of 2,000 lbs.) per year. The work of the several establishments was redistributed, and fundamental changes were made in nearly every branch of the treatment. Clausthal was made an establishment chiefly for the treatment of the ore, Lautenthal for the separation of the silver from the rich lead, and Altenau for the copper process. Andreasberg alone, on account of the peculiarly rich arsenical ores found there, retained its old works, sending, however, all its copper matte to Altenau. While these changes were in contemplation the introduction, first of the Rachette, and then of the Kast furnace, compelled some delay in order to study the performance of the new apparatus, and though years have passed, the alterations are hardly yet fully carried out.

THE WORKS AT CLAUSTHAL.

First in the series comes Clausthal where the ore is run down to metallic lead and copper matte. The process in use is one which was invented at Clausthal, and which though often derided, has probably had more influence upon the smelting of galena ores throughout the world than any other. It is the method known as precipitation. Galena, which is the main constituent of the Hartz ores consists of lead and sulphur. In all the works hitherto described in these notes the sulphur has been removed chiefly by combining it with oxygen—roasting. At Clausthal iron is used instead of oxygen. At first the metal was used direct, but it was afterwards found that a silicate rich in iron oxide served not only as well but better than the metal itself, and inasmuch as there were large stores of such silicate containing small amounts of copper and silver which could be had for the mere cost of transportation, the discovery was one of great importance. Finally another modification was made which now forms the existing mode of treatment.

One of the fundamental differences between the removal of sulphur by oxygen and by iron is that in the former case the product is volatile and passes directly out of our hands as a gas, while in the latter it is a solid, called matte. If it were possible to produce a matte containing nothing but iron and sulphur there would be absolutely no drawback to the precipitation as a process for pure lead ores, for the matte could be thrown away and the sulphur thus removed from the process. But a matte produced by smelting lead ores always contains lead, and if silver and copper are also present these metals always pass into the matte in quantity sufficient to make their extraction a necessity. The mode of this extraction is the same throughout the world. There is no substance available to the metallurgist which will take the sulphur from the iron in the matte as the iron has taken it from the lead in the ore, except one—that is oxygen—and mattes, therefore, are everywhere roasted. The oxidation of the sulphur is accompanied by oxidation of the iron, and as this is the first step toward the formation of a silicate, it is only necessary to melt the roasted matte with quartz in order to remove the oxidized iron in the form of a slag. This treatment of the matte is a serious item of expense.

The certainty that the matte will contain the copper is by no means an evil. On the contrary, were it not so the metallurgist would be puzzled to know how to separate his copper from the lead. The whole treatment of sulphides containing copper is based upon the chemical fact that copper and sulphur will in all cases unite in the furnace, provided the amount of sulphur present is not sufficient for both the iron and the copper ; the former can be removed by the addition of quartz, a slag being the result. This action is so certain that the metallurgist, who has a copper matte which has been roasted "dead," that is, has had all the sulphur removed and the copper and iron completely transformed to oxides, would have no hesitation in charging it in a furnace with an iron pyrites containing only quartz, iron and sulphur, and no copper at all. The result in all cases is that the copper unites with the sulphur and the quartz with the iron oxide.

In the Hartz, the treatment of ore and matte forms one operation. Instead of melting the ore with a slag rich in iron, to remove the sulphur, and melting the roasted matte with another slag rich in silica, to remove the iron oxide, they combine the two processes and melt the ore and the roasted matte together. As the ore contains both quartz and sulphur the oxidized iron passes partly into the slag with one and partly into a new matte with the other. The matte, therefore, makes a continuous round, being roasted and re-smelted with the ore five or six times.

It is easy to see that this is really no more nor less than a roasting process, though the roasting is transferred from the ore to a matte. There are two advantages to be obtained from this treatment. One is the less bulk of the matte to be roasted, amounting to not more than half, or at most, two-thirds the ore. The other is that the sulphides of iron are in all cases much easier and cheaper to roast than the sulphides of lead. They contain more sulphur, require less fuel, and present less liability to sintering and imperfect roasting. Other important advantages are, first, that the lead and silver having been mostly removed, the loss from volatilization is much less, and, second, that the sulphur in the matte can be utilized by making sulphuric acid from it, while the ore is useless for that purpose because it contains so little sulphur.

The ore treated at Clausthal had, according to Koch (1869), the following composition :

71.676	per cent.	lead sulphide or 62,07 lead.
0.945	do	copper sulphide 0.75 copper.
1.880	do	zinc sulphide.
0.537	do	antimony sulphide.
1.410	do	iron sulphide.
0.113	do	silver sulphide or 0.098 silver.
4.139	do	iron carbonate.
0.150	do	alumina
2.380	do	lime carbonate.
1.460	do	baryta sulphate.
0.075	do	magnesia.
15.235	do	silica.

This is a mixture of ores obtained from a great number of mines, and the occasional preponderance of ore from some one mine will sometimes alter the composition of the charges smelted for a few days. The usual composition of the charge, as at first established, may, however, be ascertained from the following quantities which were smelted during the months of July,

August, and September, 1866. The quantities are hundredweights of 110 English pounds. The proportions of hearth and rich litharge are worth noticing, for the Clausthal works use the German cupel hearth, and these are therefore the proportions in which cupel scraps are produced in treating a 62 per cent. ore, by this method:

			Per ton.
Ore	33,400 cwt.	100	2000 lb.
Roasted matte	17,565 ,,	52½	1050 ,,
Copper slag	22,248 ,,	66¾	1332 ,,
Slag from same operation	55,542 ,,	166⅓	3332 ,,
Cupel hearth	1,112 ,,	3	6 ,,
Rich litherage	624 ,,	2	3 ,,
Scraps	262 ,,	0¾	1½ ,,
Days' labor (12 h)	1,002	3⅓	3-5ths day
Coke	14,964 ,, }	47 1-5	944 lb.
Charcoal	810 ,, }		

This is therefore an expense of a three-fifths of a day's labor, and 944 pounds of coke per ton of ore. The cause of this large expense of fuel is the use of so much flux, amounting to 284 per cent. of the ore. This excessive proportion of flux is one of the peculiarities of the Hartz. Nowhere else is it used in such profusion, but innumerable attempts to reduce it there have, without exception, failed. When slag is used as a precipitating material a bulky charge is the necessary result, but even when metallic iron was the precipitating agent, 121 per cent. of slag was added to the ore. The causes of this peculiarity have never been published.

Considerable changes have been made in the above proportions, the chief of which was to cut down the amount of slag from the same operation repassed, to 75 and 70 per cent. which reduced the flux and precipitating material to 190 per cent. of the ore. The charge at one time was made up of 100 ore, 50 roasted matte, 70 copper slag, and 70 lead slag, smelted with about 43 coke. It was found, however, that with these proportions the matte became so rich in copper as to part with some of that metal to the lead. The roasted matte obtained from ore smelted with slags alone contained 3 per cent. of copper, which rose to 8 and even 9 per cent. by re-fusion with ore and the lead instead of 0.3 per cent., as formerly, contained 0.6 to 0.7 per cent. of copper. This increased the difficulty and cost of desilverization, and the proportion of roasted matte was diminished to 28 per cent. of the ore. The exact composition of the new charge I have not been able to obtain, but it is probably about the following: Ore 100, roasted matte 28, slags 150-170. After the change the copper in the matte sank to 5½ per cent., and in the lead to 0.4 and 0.5 per cent.

The products dur ng the above-mentioned three months were

	From 100 Ore
Lead, 21,380 cwt.	65⅓
Matte, 24,253 ,,	72⅔

The three methods of treatment successively used at Clausthal, have given the following results in regard to product:

With metalic iron.	With copper slag.	With roasted matte.
Lead, 54	65	65⅓ and 65
Matte, 44	55	72⅔ and 66

The simplicity of this precipitation method would recommend it in nearly all cases were it not for the large increase of cost which results from using so much flux, and the production of so much matte. The practice of adding puddle and reheating cinder to lead ores in the shaft furnace, is now so common that the business of lead smelting has, in some regions, almost become auxilliary to the manufacture of iron. Under these circumstances it is always a question whether the operation of roasting, costly in plant and in practice, cannot be supplanted by merely increasing the proportion of iron flux, and re-charging the matte formed. In those cases where ores, pure in lead and rich in silver, are smelted for the silver they contain, and there is therefore no desire to keep the lead pure, it seems probable that this method would be found decidedly advantageous.

The lead obtained is not pure. Analyses of the lead and matte given by Koch, are as follows ; although obtained by the former precipitation with copper slag, they fairly represent the same products from the present process.

	Lead.	Matte.
Antimony	0.618	0.350
Copper	0.276	4.392
Iron	0.002	55.720
Zinc	0.008	1.125
Silver	0.127	0.029
Lead	98.969	7.984
Sulphur	....	29.546
	100	99.146

The slag is maintained with great regularity between a proto-and a bi-silicate. It is rich in iron, very poor in lead, and can be thrown away at once. Only a very small portion—that which solidifies in the fore hearth—must be re-charged on account of grains of lead and matte mechanically contained in it. The following is an analysis of this ordinary slag :

Silica	43.60	Magnesia	1.56
Iron oxide	31.68	Lead oxide	0.70
Alumina	15.50	Silver oxide	0.000087
Lime	6.50		
			99.54087.

The furnaces in which the fusion takes place are of two kinds, the round or Kast furnace, and the Rachette. The round furnaces at Clausthal form an interesting series of experiments in the most recent progress of lead metallurgy. The principles which were introduced into the construction of lead furnaces by the English in Spain, 30 years ago or more, and have been modified by Pfanderheiden, Piltz, and others, have also made their way to Clausthal. Five round furnaces of various dimensions and construction are found there. One of the peculiarities of the Clausthal system of smelting is that the ore must be in the form of powder, and this formerly caused so much dust that from 5 to 8 per cent. was taken from the dust chambers. This gave rise to a very unusual mode of building the furnaces. A row of heavy brick piers was built, and the intervening spaces arched over. On these arches was raised a line of dust chambers, which not being intended to condense volatilized lead, but merely to give the

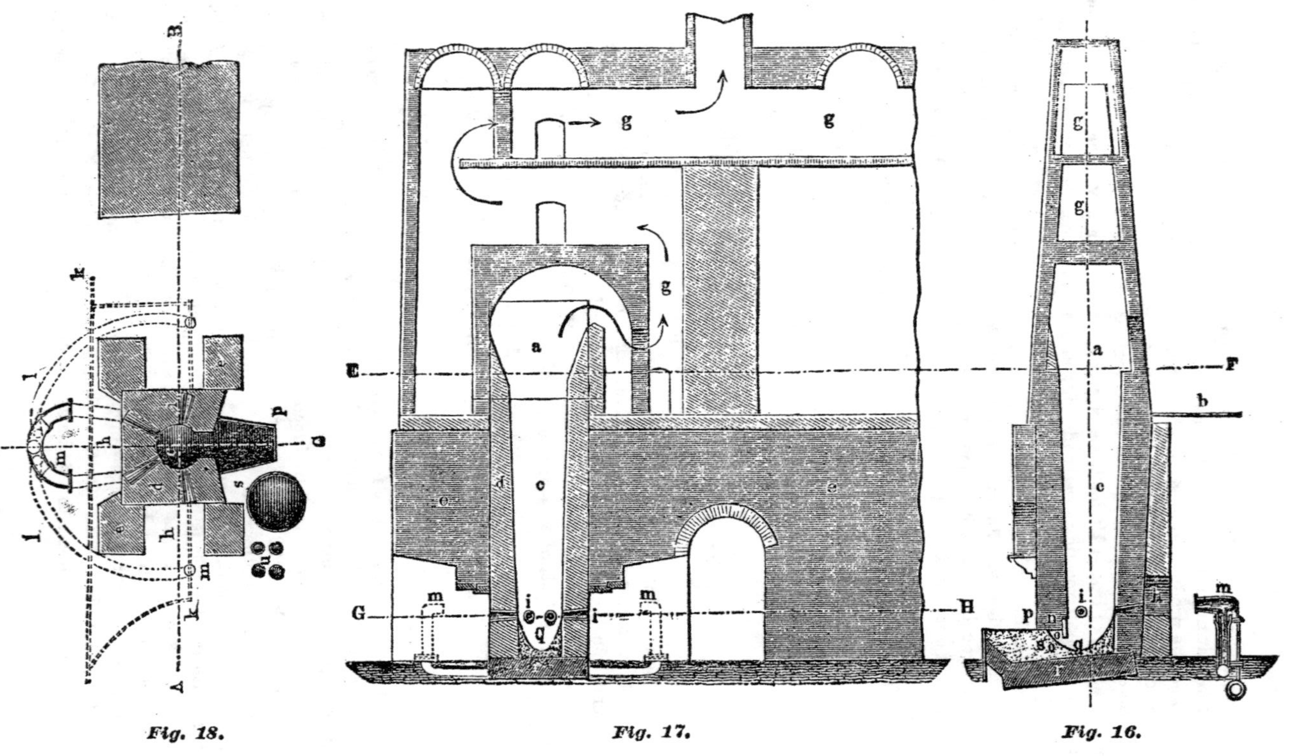

Fig. 18.

Fig. 17.

Fig. 16.

fine dust opportunity to settle, could be placed immediately over the furnaces. But the result of this mode of construction was to place a limit to the size of the furnace which could be built between two of the piers, and when the new doctrines in furnace building began to spread Mr. KAST, director at the smelting works at Clausthal, had to experiment to ascertain what were the smallest diameters that would prevent the dust from flying out of his furnaces. At first a furnace 3 feet in diameter at the tuyeres and 4 feet at the top was built, but the amount of dust was still excessive. Then the diameter at the mouth was increased to 4½ feet, which caused a reduction of the flue dust to 2 per cent. The slowness of the ascending current of gas in the upper part of the furnace also affects very favorably the utilization of the coke, and the amount of material run through in a day. The following table gives a comparison of the four round furnaces with a Rachette. All of the round furnaces have the same diameter at the tuyeres, 3 feet, and the same height, 21 feet. The diameter of the Rachette at the tuyeres is also 3 feet.

Diameter at mouth.	Coke per 100 ore.	Flue dust.	Time to smelt 11,000 lbs. ore.
No. 1....4ft. 2in.	42.39	2.8 per cent.	73.2 hours.
No. 2....4ft. 8in.	41.85	2.1 "	71.8 "
No. 3....5ft. 0in.	41.74	1.7 "	71.2 "
No. 4....5ft. 3in.	41.62	1.1 "	60.2 "
Rachette..4ft. 9in.	44.3	1 "	93.2 "

The round furnaces, called also Kast furnaces, after the Director of the works, do not differ from the general type of modern lead furnaces, except that, being built between piers of masonry, they are not approachable on all sides. They are made with fore hearth, over the dam of which the slag runs without cessation. The number of tuyeres ranges from 4 to 7.

Like so many lead furnaces in Europe, these are built of ordinary red brick, only a few fire brick being placed around the tuyeres, and these are in fact often omitted. These furnaces have made an uninterrupted campaign of 2 or 3 years, a result which is due to the accuracy with which the composition of the slag is calculated and maintained. The ore and flux are spread out in layers upon each other on the floor at the furnace mouth, and charged equally over the whole surface of the furnace, the coke being spread out in the same way. The pressure of air is 10 to 12 lines of mercury.

Figures 12 to 14 give sections of the Kast furnaces. The dimensions of one are

Height..........................	20ft.
Diameter at mouth....	5ft.
Do. at tuyeres..............	3ft.
Do. at sole..................	2ft. 4in.
Number of tuyeres...........	4
Pressure of blast.............	11—14 lines of mercury.

They are open at the mouth, having no hopper nor cylinder. The ore and coke are spread evenly over the surface, the ore being thrown from wooden troughs, and the coke from flat baskets. The charges for 24 hours are always made up in the morning, so that at night nothing but tapping the furnace and throwing the slag off the slag-run takes place. All furnaces at Clausthal have a fore hearth, over the edge of which the slag runs, passing down a narrow inclined

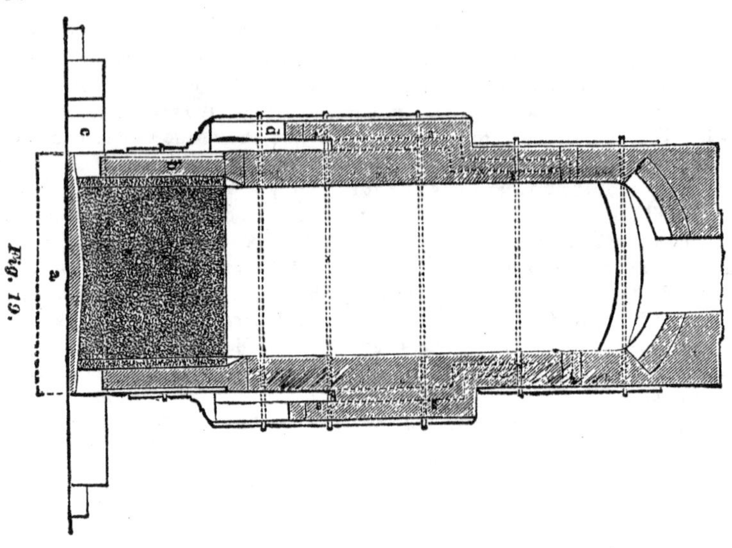

Fig. 19.

RACHETTE FURNACE AT CLAUSTHAL.

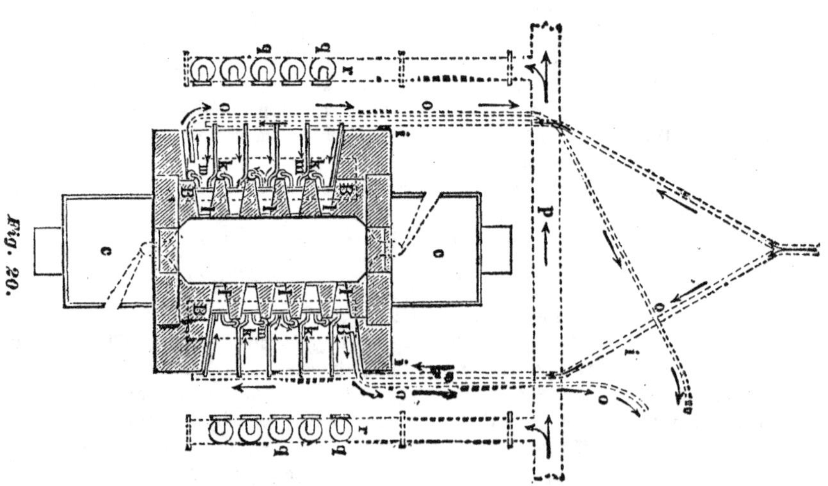

Fig. 20.

bank made of brasque. It solidifies on this, and is thrown to one side by the workman who wields a two-pronged fork. The lead is not tapped f om the body of the furnace, but from the front hearth where it collects. This front hearth is formed inside of an iron box projecting from the furnace, and in the side of this box is the tap.

In addition to these Kast furnaces Clausthal possesses a Piltz of the same pattern as those at Freiburg, but w th some judicious alterations in the method of suspension. It is octagonal, 24 feet high, 4ft. 8in. diameter at the tuyeres, and 6ft. 8in. at the mouth. The 8 water tuyeres are 15 inches above the slag spouts. It was attempted to run this furnace with a closed hearth, but outside modifications do not seem to succeed in the Hartz, and it was found impossible to produce a fusible slag. The furnace was accordingly narrowed to 4ft. 2in. at the tuyeres, and fitted with a front hearth. It is now in successful operation.

The Rachette furnaces were for a long time the best that Clausthal possessed, but they seem to offer no advantages over the round furnaces, while they are not only more costly to build, but also are subject to a patent right. Their form is

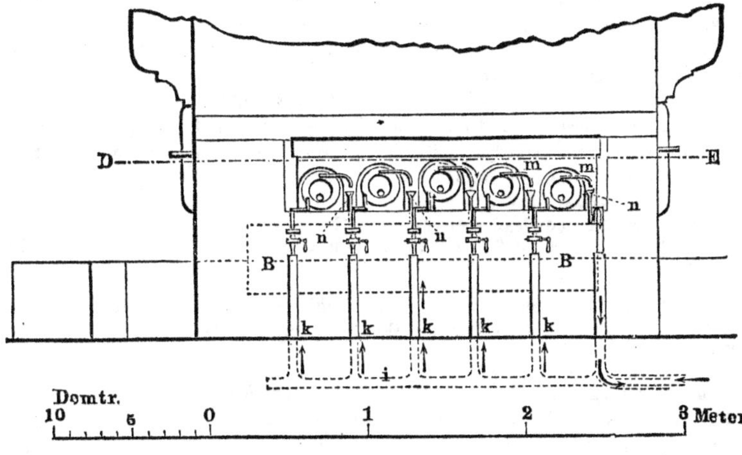

Fig. 21.

shown in figures 15 to 18. Figure 15 shows a vertical section of the furnace through the longer axis ; fig. 16 is a horizontal section, though the tuyeres, fig. 17, shows the tuyeres in place, and fig. 18 gives a horizontal section and end view of a tuyere.

The Rachette furnace is a construction designed to obtain great capacity, without making the diameter greater than twice the throw of the blast. To that end it is made rectangular, and long and narrow. Tuyeres are placed on each of the long sides, and throw their air through the furnace in its narrowest direction ; and the form of the furnace is such that any number of tuyeres can be used by merely lengthening the furnace. Usually five on a side is the number. Formerly the ends had no tuyeres, but it having been observed that scaffolds and accretions collected only on the ends, these have also been furnished with

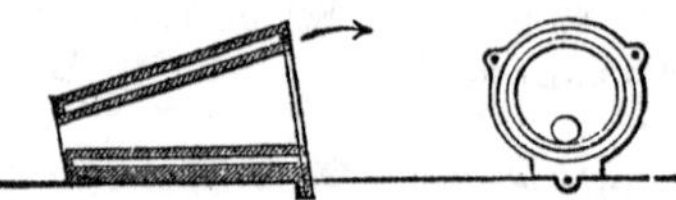

Fig. 22.

tuyeres, and with good effect. There is a tap at each end which requires a double set of men at the bottom. The main dimensions of the Altenau Rachette furnace, the first built in the Hartz, are given below ; they have not been materially changed in any of the newer ones :

Height	19 feet	6 inches.
Width at tuyeres	2 ,,	11 ,,
Width at top	4 ,,	6 ,,
Length	7 ,,	4 ,,
Distance between tuyeres	1 ,,	4 ,,

It is an excellent furnace and smelts 16,500 lb. of ore, or 44,000 lb. of charge in 24 hours with about 5,500 lb. coke. The increased width of the throat keeps the loss by dust down to a minimum, provided the pressure of blast does not exceed 10 or 12 lines of mercury.

THE WORKS AT LAUTENTHAL.

The lead is all desilvered at Lautenthal by the zinc and steam process, which, however, differs very greatly in its details from the system pursued at other works. The operations in the process are :

1. Fusion and treatment with zinc.
2. Treatment of poor lead with steam, under a hood, to remove the zinc.
3. Treatment of the poor lead with steam and admission of air, to remove the antimony.
4. Casting the purified lead.
5. Treatment of the rich crusts, or alloy, with steam, to remove the zinc.
6. Cupellation of the rich lead resulting from 5, with addition of the rich oxides to extract their silver.
7. Treatment of the poor oxides.

Treatment with Zinc.—The kettles used are old Pattinson kettles, of 5 feet 6½ inches diameter and 2 feet 10 inches depth. Each holds 27,500 lb. of lead, and three are worked together, forming a battery. The two outer kettles are charged with 27½ tons (of 2,000 lb.) of lead, which is melted down in about six hours, when an *abzug*, or lead containing enough copper, iron, etc., to make its point of fusion higher than that of pure metal, is taken off and cast in moulds. Each of the end kettles, then receives 49½ lb. zinc. The object of making this first charge so small is to concentrate the gold, of which the lead contains a very minute proportion, in a small quantity of silver. It is a peculiarity of the process that silver is not taken up except in a small quantity, until the gold and copper have been removed. The result of this first charge is a crust which contains all the copper and gold, without being much richer in silver than the original work lead. In spite of this decided concentration, the silver made from this crust contains only 0.12 to 0.20 per cent. of gold. Still the latter metal pays for its separation.

When the zinc charge has melted, the bath is stirred by two men at each kettle for twenty-five minutes, the stirrer being a broad, flat and long-handled iron disc, pierced with holes. The metal is then cooled until a crust of about 1½ inches thickness forms on top. It is a matter of importance to so manage the cooling that it shall take place mainly from the surface, in order to prevent the formation of a thick crust on the bottom of the kettle, for this crust would contain zinc and silver. To avoid this the fire is merely covered with ashes. The top crust is thrown into the middle kettle, and when this is completed a new charge of 258½ lb. zinc is made to each outside vessel, and the fires are freshened. The stirring in, cooling down, and skimming are repeated, and the last charge of 77 lb. zinc is then made, and the same operation gone through with. The time consumed in completing a change is about as follows: Drawing abzug, 30 minutes; melting, 1—1½ hours; total, 6—7 hours. The desilverization of 27½ tons of lead requires about thirty hours.

The middle kettle is now heated, the bath stirred, cooled and skimmed, the crust being a concentration of the three crusts taken from the other two kettles. This is cast in moulds. From 20 to 40 lb. of zinc are added to the bath, and the above operations are repeated. If necessary, a second charge of zinc is made.

According to the above the zinc charge amounts to 1¼ per cent of the lead. The crusts, do not contain all the zinc, but fully one-half is left in the poor lead. The removal of this zinc has been the most difficult problem in the whole process of desilverization, and though the poor lead can now be treated without difficulty, no direct and simple method of separating the zinc from the rich crusts has yet been found, unless the costly mode of distillation is excepted.

Dezincing the poor lead.—The three kettles now contain poor lead, which is dezinced by blowing superheated steam at 15 lb. pressure through the bath, by means of a bent pipe, two inches in diameter, running to the bottom. A sheet iron hood communicating with a large pipe is bolted down on the kettle and the joint is luted. The lead is kept at a little below cherry red, and is steamed for four hours to remove the zinc, and for two hours more to remove the antimony, air being admitted by opening the door of the hood. Inasmuch as the antimony is not carried over with the rich crust, the middle kettle is steamed to remove the zinc alone. In this operation the temperature is a point of great importance. If too low, a longer time is required, and the amount of oxides formed is increased. If too high, the kettles are rapidly destroyed. At the right temperature 0·7 per cent. of zinc and 1 per cent. of antimony can be removed in the time given.

The object of passing the steam through the bath is to oxidize the zinc, but a good deal of lead is also oxidized, and the oxide first formed is fluid, but it gradually becomes powdery and "dry." The oxides from the end kettles are yellow, but those formed in the middle kettle are greenish, showing a preponderance of zinc. Perfect dryness of the oxides is a sign that all the zinc has been removed. Other tests are to cast a small assay in a scorifier from time to time, until no star forms in the center upon cooling. The star would indicate the presence of antimony. The kettle is also left exposed to the air a while, without steam, after the oxides have been removed. If a clear red litharge forms, the lead is pure. Another test for zinc is to take a ladle-full, scrape the surface, while hot, with a piece of wood, and if the silky appearance is gone the zinc has been removed. When the tests show the lead to be free from both zinc and antimony, the lead is ladled into moulds, and forms the "Refined Hartz lead." It is so nearly pure as to contain from 99·983 to 99·987 per cent. lead.

The dezincing of the rich crust presents more difficulties. The withdrawal of oxygen from the steam by the zinc leaves a gas so highly charged with hydrogen as to be violently explosive when the hot gas comes in contact with the air. In dezincing the poor lead, the deoxydation of the steam is quite imperfect, and the resulting gas never gives alarming explosions. But the rich crusts contain 5 or 6 per cent. of zinc, and severe explosions of the gas have occurred. These are, however, now completely prevented by turning steam direct into the hood before allowing air to enter it.

The products now consist of: (1) refined lead ready for market; (2) rich lead containing about 1½ per cent. silver which is cupelled in a German hearth. (3) Poor oxides free from antimony, and others containing antimony. The former are washed on a sleeping table which separates them into two qualities. Of these one consists of metallic lead and lead oxide, containing about 85 per cent. of the metal; it is reduced to second quality metal. The remainder, containing much zinc, is of a yellow color and is sold as paint. The oxides containin antimony are melted with other similar products to hard lead. (4) Rich oxides. These are placed upon the bath in the cupel furnace, the heat being raised to the highest limit. The silver passes into the lead, some lead being oxidized in the exchange. A slag, consisting of zinc oxide, lead oxide and metallic lead, remains and is drawn off. It contains about 50 ounces silver to the ton and is reduced with rich litharge to metal which passes a second time through the desilverization process. To have a successful imbibition, or absorption of silver by the lead in the cupel hearth, it is necessary to keep the rich oxides from being too dry. With lead, such as is produced in the Hartz—containing 38 ounces to the ton—the oxides are in the right proportion when they form 8 to 10 per cent. of the desilvered lead.

WEDDING and BRÆUNNING give the following summary of the results obtained by this process in 1869. The German centner of 110 lb. English weight is here given as cwt.

MATERIAL AND PRODUCTS.

	WEIGHT.		PERCENTAGE.	
	SILVER. lb.	LEAD. lb.	SILVER.	LEAD.
Charged: 22,053 cwt. work lead	3168⅓	22,021⅓		
Produced: 3,525½ lb. crude silver, containing fine silver	3243½		102·372	
Refined Hartz lead		18,803¾		85·389
Second quality lead		1,907⅔		8·662
Hard lead		489½		2 223
Oxides containing no silver		55¼		0·250
Merchantable litharge 64 cwt.		58¾		0.267
Total	3233½	211,315	102·362	96·791
Various products not worked up: 452 cwt.		392¼		1·781
Total			102·372	98 592

It is certainly remarkable that the intermediate products still in treatment, consisting of hearth, scraps, litharge, abstrich, and impure lead obtained in liquating the hard lead, should amount to only 22½ tons or 1·781 per cent. of the lead treated. The second quality lead is made from the washed oxides mentioned above, the scraps formed in ladling the first quality metal from the kettle and other products free from silver. It is blown with steam to remove the antimony and then cast. Its only impurity is a small proportion of copper. The hard lead is obtained by smelting the oxides containing antimony, and this also is blown with steam to remove the zinc and copper. Thus the steam process is now used for the refining of all kinds, and by its use the numerous operations which made up the old process of cupellation and refining by air have been entirely superseded.

In ladling out the refined lead, an assay weighing about ½ lb. is cast for every 8 pigs of lead. When 5000 pigs have been cast, these assays are melted together, and some pounds are cast and sent to the laboratory for analysis. The first of the following analyses is from the lead produced at Lautenthal in 1870 up to the month of August, and represents 20,465 pigs or about 1575 tons. The other is from 1193 tons of lead refined at Altenau, where refining was still in operation in that year. Each analysis is the mean of 4 made upon 1400 grammes in one case, and 1500 grammes in the other. It is noteworthy that although refined at different and widely separated establishments, and made from work lead of very different composition in regard to impurity, the refined lead shows a difference of only 4-1000 of a per cent., that from Altenau, where the copper ores and matte are worked, showing a small excess of impurity. This similarity of composition is a proof of the method with which the operations are carried out.

Lead	99·983139	99·987560
Copper	0·001413	0·002022
Antimony	0·005698	0·003335
Bismuth	0·005487	0·003650
Silver	0·000460	0 000721
Iron	0·002289	0·001229
Zinc	0·000834	0·000776
Nickel	0·000680	0·000707
	100·	100·

In regard to the bismuth present in the above, it is worthy of remark that steam has no effect upon this metal, which remains with the lead. This circumstance, which has been developed only within a few years, is a matter of great importance to works which, like Freiberg, make considerable quantities of bismuth from intermediate products, which would be lost were it not concentrated in those products. Pattinson's process effects this concentration, and this is another reason why that system of concentration, now so generally rejected, should be retained at Freiberg.

The purity which now distinguishes the Harz lead has not been obtained without much trouble and study. Compared with the lead obtained from cupellation, the Pattinson, salt-and-poling and steam processes have yielded a product which has shown an advancing purity.

THE COPPER PROCESS AT ALTENAU.

When the matte is withdrawn from the ore fusion it contains about eight per cent. copper and seven per cent. lead. It is roasted in a square kiln, twenty feet high, four feet square at the bottom, and 5×4 feet at the top. The matte is broken into pieces, 1 or 1½ inches square. Only the upper part of the kiln is hot, the fire not sinking below 3 feet from the mouth, while the remaining 9 feet serve as a regenerator to heat the ascending air, a process which of course cools the matte. Two doors at the mouth are used for charging ; two others are placed two feet under them for the purpose of loosening the charge, and finally there are two more on a level with the sole, to allow for discharging. With good management of the draft the kiln burns for weeks. If too much air enters, the combustion may be sufficiently strong to sinter the charge together, or, allowed to increase still further, enough cold air to put the fire out may enter. The matte, which contains about 22 per cent, of sulphur, is reduced to 12 per cent. by two roastings in the kiln. The kilns are connected with sulphuric acid chambers, and no difficulty has occurred in utilizing the sulphur of the matte in this way. After the second kiln roasting, the matte is piled in a low heap and roasted with the addition of brush fuel to 6 per cent. sulphur. It is then smelted in low, square furnaces, about 9 feet in height, 1 foot 8 inches × 3 feet 4 inches square at the bottom, and 2 × 3 feet 10 inches at the top. The introduction of sloping sides has been found advantageous. Three water tuyeres are placed in the back wall, the piers between which the furnaces stand, preventing their introduction at the sides.

The charge consists of 100 roasted matte and about 93 slag, partly siliceous slag from the ore fusion, and partly matte slag repassed.

The products are (1) Lead containing 0·19 per cent. silver and more copper, iron, zinc, antimony, etc., than the metal from the ore ; (2) Copper matte, the composition of which is about :

Sulphur	21·6	per cent.
Iron	39·2	"
Copper	23·7	"
Lead	15·0	"
Silver	0·057	"

(3) Slag containing 2 per cent. lead, and 0·002 per cent. silver. When copper slag was used as a precipitating material, the mattes from this fusion contained only 11 per cent. of copper, and required another roasting and fusion before entering the copper process. Now this is unnecessary.

The treatment of the copper matte consists in enriching it by repeated roasting and fusion with siliceous material, to black copper containing 95 per cent. of that metal. This is granulated, treated with hot sulphuric acid, the copper sulphate crystallized out, and the rich residues smelted to obtain their silver and gold.

The copper matte is roasted in the kilns described above. Fusions take place in what are called in Germany "spectacle" furnaces. They are 10 ft. 8 in. high, have a section of from 18 to 36 in. × 3 ft. 4 in., and owe their name to the fact that they have two reception basins in front. They have one tuyere each, use

250 cubic feet of air per minute at a pressure of 7 to 9 lines of mercury, and smelt from 9,300 to 10,000 lb. of roasted matte in 24 hours. The composition of the charge is the same as in smelting lead matte, except that instead of ore slag a siliceous slag from another operation in the copper process is charged. A very basic slag is produced which eats away the furnace wall so rapidly that the campaigns do not exceed 24 to 30 days. The roasting and fusion is repeated five times, and KUHLEMANN gives the following summary of the charges and products:

FUSION NUMBER		1	2	3	4	5
Charge: Roasted copper matte	cwt.	5075	2400	1050	300	125
Siliceous slag	"	3787	1801	788	225	95
Slag from same operation	"	988	480	210	60	35
Fuel: Coke	"	1375	715	365	95	30
Peat } for warming	pieces	8590	3000	1400	750	250
Charcoal } furnace	cu. ft.	10	—	—	10	—
Matte melted in 24 hours	cwt.	86¾	81⅓	100	66⅔	83⅓
Coke used per 100 cwt. matte	"	27	29·8	34·7	29·4	—
Products: Work lead=0·38 p.c. silv.	"	40	—	—	—	—
Black copper	"	20	408	384	125	44
Matte	"	2400	1050	300	125	60
Slag	"	6100	2600	1160	290	140
100 cwt. matte give Work lead	"	0·79	—	—	—	—
Black copper	"	0·40	17·0	36·57	41·66	35·20
Matte	"	47·30	43·75	28·57	41·66	48·0
COMPOSITION OF THE PRODUCTS.						
Black copper: Copper	per ct.	40	70	93·5	94	95
Lead	"	55	25	1	2	2
Silver	"	0·265	0·22	0·160	0·100	0·085
Matte: Copper	"	40	66	70	73	73
Lead	"	9	5	3	2	3
Silver	"	0·0725	0·078	0·065	0·045	0·030
Slag: Copper	"	1·	1·	1	1·5	1·25
Lead	"	0·75	1·5	0·75	1·25	1
Silver	"	0·00093	0·00125	0·00063	0·00063	0·00063

The charge in each fusion was therefore

Roasted matte....................100
Siliceous slag.................... 75
Slag from same operation........... 20

and the time required for its fusion was about 28 hours. To pass 100 cwt. of the first matte through the 5 fusions in succession requires about 51 cwt. coke, 49 hours actual smelting time, and in the 5 fusions 179 cwt. matte will be treated. The data above given are, however, only a portion of the expenses. Counting them as 100 we have to add as follows:

Expenses in fusion,	for labor, 100	for fuel, 100
" roasting,	" 45	" 28
" removing slag,	" 13½	
" transporting matte	" 25	
" general expenses..........	97	

The entire cost will be about 165 per cent. of the cost of labor and fuel consumed in the fusions.

The slag used as siliceous flux had the following composition:

Silica	34·67	Lead oxide	1·07
Alumina	4·38	Iron oxide	48·25
Lime	3 53	Sulphur	1·25
Manganese oxide	2·00		
Zinc oxide	2·89		98·64

The following analysis of the slag from the 5th fusion is a fair representation of the same product from all the operations:

Silica	30·994	Lime	4·314
Antimony oxide	0·196	Magnesia	0·253
Iron oxide	58·605	Alumina	5·732
Copper oxide	0·933		
Lead oxide	0·021		101·048

The preceding tables show that a certain amount of black copper is made in each fusion. That from the first operation is, however, small in quantity and quite impure, containing a good deal of lead and silver. The total amount of black copper from all the operations is 19½ per cent. of the first matte. The greater part of it is obtained in the 2d and 3d fusions.

The black copper from all the fusions is mixed with purchased copper containing silver, and "blown" in a reverberatory furnace. The mixture contains from 0 16 to 0·20 per cent. silver and 80 to 83 per cent. copper. The furnace is a cupel hearth of the old form. That is to say, the roof is fixed and must therefore be high enough to permit the workman to enter the furnace to make the hearth. This is formed of clay and coke screenings, with a border of mergel, and is nearly 10 feet in diameter. In front of the furnace is a water basin in which the copper is granulated as it comes out. From 50 to 53 cwt. of black copper is charged, melted in 5 hours, a "carcase" or alloy of higher fusing point than the black copper is drawn off from the surface, and air is blown upon the bath, at first in a feeble current but at length at the rate of 250 cubic feet a minute. Lead, iron, zinc, cobalt, nickel, antimony and some copper are oxidized and, drawing silica from the hearth, form a slag which is drawn or run off from the surface. After blowing 10 or 11 hours the refined copper is tapped and granulated. It contains 91 to 97 per cent. copper and 0·20 to 0·40 per cent. silver. The analysis of a black copper made in this way in 1870 was as follows:

Iron	0·070	Copper	95·00
Lead	2·71	Antimony	1·53
Nickel, cobalt, zinc	0·048	Arsenic	trace
Silver	0·30		99·658

In the Notes on Freiberg, the necessity of excluding iron from the matte which was to be treated with acid, and the means used to accomplish this, were spoken of. It will be observed that the same result is reached at Altenau by repeated roastings and fusions, and finally, by an oxidizing fusion of the resulting black copper.

In addition to the black copper, two products are obtained. One is the carcase drawn off from the bath immediately after fusion. It contains 15 to 20 per cent. silica, 5 per cent. nickel oxide, 3½ per cent. cobalt oxide, 10 to 12 per cent. copper oxide, and 35 to 40 per cent lead oxide. The amount produced is small, but when enough has accumulated, it will be smelted with arsenical ores and heavy spar to produce a speise rich in nickel. The other product is the very impure litharge obtained by blowing the black copper, and containing 51½ per cent. lead, 16 per cent. copper, and 0·016 per cent silver. It is mixed with the hearth, which is saturated with the same product, and smelted to a black copper containing a great deal of lead and some silver. This is liquated to remove the lead, and then blown like the ordinary black copper, furnishing, however, a much greater proportion of side products.

The following are the details of the operations in 1869:

Number of charges		74	
Black copper	cwt.	3,225¾	100
Products, Granulated copper	"	2,201	68¼
Carcase	"	63	2
Litharge	"	976	30¼
Faggots		39,450	1220
or Bituminous coal	cwt.		42

The faggots mentioned are now replaced by bituminous coal, and experience shows that 1,000 faggots are equal to about 34½ cwt. coal.

The granulated copper is treated with dilute sulphuric acid, by which the copper, iron, nickel, and cobalt are dissolved, leaving a residue composed of gold, silver and arsenic in the metallic state, lead sulphate and basic antimony sulphate. The vats in which the solution is accomplished, are 4 feet high and 3 feet 4 inches in diameter. They are lined with lead, and have a perforated false bottom 4 inches above the floor of the vat. Great care is taken in filling the vat, for it is important to have the mass of granules as open and porous as possible. While copper oxide dissolves readily in dilute sulphuric acid, the metal itself requires hot concentrated acid for its solution. At Altenau the metal is oxidized by allowing the acid in the vat to run out, the air filling the spaces between the granules, which, being hot and moist with acid, oxidize, and the oxide is taken up by the succeeding charge of acid. To ensure the complete access of air, the layer of copper must not be more than 40 inches thick, so that the vat holds about 2,200 lb. It is filled up as often as the surface falls 10 inches below the normal level, which occurs two or three times a week. The vat is cleaned out once in eight or ten weeks. One vat suffices to dissolve about 93 lb. of copper per day, yielding about 360 lb. of vitriol

The sulphuric acid is taken direct from the chambers, and marks 48 to 50 deg. B. It is thinned to 32 deg. B. in a tank heated by steam to 175 deg. F. The diluted acid is thrown on the copper, by means of a lead pipe furnished with a rose, every half hour. The acid runs through rapidly, but has time to dissolve the oxides formed, and the force of its flow is sufficient to carry along the fine insoluble residues. This is an important point, for without this removal of the residues not only will the granules be covered with an insoluble coat, but the interstices will also be filled up. A turbid liquor discharging from the spout in the bottom of the vat is therefore the sign of a good operation. This spout being left open, air draws through the mass as soon as the interstices are free from acid, the draft being aided by the heat of the copper, derived from the acid.

A high temperature hastens the operation, but is liable to cause solution of the silver. The six vats at Altenau discharge into a trough 360 feet long, where the warm solution deposits first the insoluble residue it has brought along, and then, as it cools, the copper sulphate crystallizes out. The trough is 30 inches wide and 7 inches deep. The mother liquor, which is still very acid, is raised to the diluting tank by means of a Gifford's injector, made of lead.

The succeeding operations are for the purification of the copper vitriol and the reduction of the residue. To accomplish the former, the raw vitriol is dissolved in hot mother liquor, the solution marking 28 deg. B. It is filtered through granulated lead, and then through granulated copper to remove by precipitation any dissolved silver, and also to retain residues that were too fine to settle in the trough. In 1½ months the lead and copper have taken up 1 per cent. of silver, and are removed. The copper vitriol is crystallized in vats lined with lead, and with strips of the same metal hanging in the liquor. The vats are emptied every eleven days, and the crystals dried. Their composition is :

Iron	0·0107	per cent.
Antimony..................	0·0123	"
Arsenic	0·0064	"
Zinc......................	trace	
Nickel	0·0006	"
Silver....................	trace	
Total impurity......	0·0300	per cent.

Nine dissolving vats and three re-dissolving pans treat 2,500 cwt. of copper yearly, producing about 9,000 cwt. of vitriol. Nine men are employed in 24 hours, five by day and four by night.

The argentiferous residues are thrown into a tank, washed, dried, and made up into balls with an equal quantity of litharge. An analysis shows that they contain :

Silver............	3.10	Antimony............	14.33
Gold	0.004	Arsenic	3.15
Copper	7.15	Sulphuric Acid........	16.67
Lead	34.46		

The copper is partly sulphate and partly fine particles which are washed down by the acid. The subsequent treatment consists in smelting the mixed litharge and residue in a shaft furnace and cupelling the metal. Care is taken to treat all the products by themselves, as they are very rich in silver. The details of the foregoing operations are

I.—Vitriol Manufacture.

Granulated copper treated................	cwt.	2305	100
Copper vitriol produced	"	8239	357⅓
Raw vitriol..............................	"	392	17
Argentiferous residues (one-half litharge)..	"	342	14⅜
Sulphuric acid consumed, 50-60 deg. B....	"	4373	189⅗
Coal	"	8336	361½
In twenty-four hours copper treated.......	"	6·4	
" " vitriol made.........	"	22·88	

II.—Smelting the Residues.

Charge :	Residues	cwt.	342	100
	Litharge and hearth	"	674½	197¼
	Iron	"	7	2
	Siliceous slag	"	508	148½
	Basic slag	"	372	108¾
Products :	Rich work lead	"	481	140⅔
	Rich copper matte	"	49	14⅓
	Slag	"	1347	394
Coke		"	290	84¾

Thirty cwt. residues were smelted in 24 hours.

III.—Cupellation.

Charge :	Work lead	cwt.	536	100
Products:	Auriferous silver	lb.	424	} 105¼
	Ordinary silver	"	150	
	Abstrich	cwt.	114	21¼
	Litharge	"	339	63¼
	Hearth	"	148	27⅔
Fuel :	Faggots		2862	495

It will be observed that while 100 parts pure copper should yield 393·37 parts vitriol, the product from the impure copper used was 357·29 parts of merchantable vitriol, and 17 parts retained by the intermediate products, a total of 374·29, or about 95 per cent. Nor does the use of sulphuric acid correspond with the theoretical requirements, being 189·65 nstead of 154·57, as required. The difference is due to the fact that the acid used is really below 66 deg., and that the intermediate solutions hold a considerable amount of acid, not accounted for.

Labor averages 54 cents a day, and the coal, which is of good quality and bears a high charge for transportation, costs about $4.80 per ton (2240 lb.), and coke $6. Under these conditions, the items in the manufacture of vitriol bore the following proportions:

	Vitriol Manufacture.	Treatment of Residues.
Sundries	8	7
Labor	20	32¾
Acid	52	—
Coal	20	—
Coke		34¼
Wood		17
General Expenses		9
	100	100

The cost of treating 100 cwt. of 40 per cent. copper matte was, in 1869, 301 thalers 7½ sgr., or (thaler=72 cents gold) $216.90. While this is apparently high, it is to be remembered that much of it is due to the acid employed, which, however, does not go to waste, but is sold as a part of the finished product. Compared with the old liquation process, the present system extracts about eight per cent. more silver, and is in every respect superior.

The results of the treatment described above are very remarkable in respect to the percentage of the different metals obtained from the ore. Koch gave the production by the "combined" process or fusion of roasted matte with the ore as,

Silver, 102·5 per cent. of assayed value of ore.
Lead, 100·8 " " "
Copper, 100·3 " " "

Thus the smelting operations gave more metal than the assay calls for, a circumstance that is, of course, due to the fact that losses take place in making the assay which are not accounted for. WEDDING & BRÆUNNING found that by the desilverization process now in use the amount of silver extracted is 2·372 per cent. more than the assay shows to be present in the lead. If, however, the silver absorbed by the cupel is allowed for at 3 per cent., there would be a real loss of 0·628 per cent. of silver. Similar corrections would make still larger differences between the apparent and the real extraction of the other metals. But the Hartz process is, nevertheless, remarkable for the closeness with which it works to the assay. The exact loss is not known, but it is less than 4 per cent. of lead, and probably less than 1 per cent. silver. These results are especially significant from the fact that the Hartz works treat unroasted ore, and they sustain the view of PLATTNER, who looked upon the process of roasting as one decidedly wasteful of metal, by volatilization. Another cause of the small loss is the persistence with which intermediate products of only moderate richness are reduced to metal and again desilvered, a method which would not always pay in America.

But the close extraction of metal is not the only proof of good work in the Hartz. The directors of the various smelting works there are the first to solve the problem of utilizing the sulphur in galena for the manufacture of acid. Pure galena contains only about 13 per cent. of sulphur, a quantity too small to be utilized with profit. It is only by concentrating this element in a matte that it can be made to give sufficiently concentrated fumes for oxidation in the lead chambers. But this matte usually contains so much lead that it sinters at a low heat, a difficulty that has heretofore barred the way to its use in kilns, as a source of acid. The introduction of the precipitation by slag taught the Clausthal metallurgists that it is possible to make a matte poor in lead from lead ores. It seems to be probable that precipitation is more thoroughly performed when the ore trickles through a bath of slag rich in iron than when it is brought in contact with metallic iron, even when the heat is sufficient to melt the latter. The introduction of precipitation by slag increased the amount of matte produced, but it decreased its percentage of lead from 40 to 7 or 10 per cent., and the latter limits have been retained in the matte from the combined fusion of ore and matte. In addition to the metals they contain, the Hartz ores, which are true galenas, are now made to yield a part of their sulphur as acid.

I have found it impossible to obtain any trustworthy calculations of the cost of the above treatment. The following is probably not very far from the truth, rather under than over. The calculation is made on one European ton, 1000 k= 2200 lb.:

Ore and lead matte fusions, 2200 lb. ore............	$7.82
Treatment of copper matte, 110 lb................	2.60
Treatment of lead matte, 1227 lb..................	2.76
	$13.18 (coin)

The products are about as follows, allowing the production of copper to form 1 per cent. of the ore:

Lead..............1210 lb., or a loss of about 1½ per cent.
Sulphate of copper, 78⅔ lb.
Silver................2 lb.; loss supposed to be about ¾ oz.

Skilled labor costs in the Hartz from 48 to 54 cents coin, and ordinary labor, say from 36 to 43 cents. Coke costs $6.70 per ton; soft coal, $4.80; a "schock," or 60 faggots of wood (equal to 225 lb. soft coal in use), 96 cents; and the copper slag used as a flux in the ore fusion is brought from Oker at a cost of 96 cents a ton.

THE OPERATIONS IN 1871.

Doctor WEDDING contributes every year to the *Preussische Zeitschrift für Berg, Hütten und Salinen Wesen*, which is the official mining journal of the Prussian Government, an account of the current experiments and improvements in the smelting works of that Government. His report of the progress made during 1871 gives so much relating to the Hartz, that I take from it the following details:

The mines of the Upper Hartz yielded in 1871: 154,622 tons (2204 lb.) of ore, which by concentration was reduced to 13,546 tons of smelting ore, having a composition similar to that given above. The smelting ore, therefore, formed 8·7 per cent. of the mine ore, and the latter, as it was hoisted from the mine, must have averaged about as follows: Lead, 5·4 per cent.; Copper, 0·065 per cent.; Silver, 0·0085 per cent., or 3½ oz. to the ton. During that year the smelting works treated 13,911 tons of home and 497 tons of foreign ore, and produced 7,930 tons lead, 47½ tons litharge, 41·58 lb. gold, and 37,523 lb. silver. Of this ore, 9,150 tons were smelted at Clausthal, seven furnaces being used for the first fusion. Five of them were round furnaces, of the KAST and PILTZ pattern, three having 4 tuyeres, one 5, and one 8 tuyeres. Two RACHETTE furnaces, each with 12 tuyeres, were also in operation.

The charge consisted of	100	ore,
" "	51	roasted matte,
" "	67	copper slag,
" "	43	matte slag,
" "	47	slag from the same operation,
308		
	1·2	scraps,
	1·0	flue dust,
	0·5	lead scraps.
2·7		
310·7		

The fuel, including the small coke used in making the "gestübbe," which forms the fore hearth, and also that used to warm the furnaces, amounted to

	45·17	coke,
	2·55	charcoal,
47·72		

or 15⅓ per cent. of the total charge, and 47¾ per cent. of the ore.

The products were:

	58·77	wo k lead,
	76·09	matte.
124·86		

If the amount of matte charged is deducted from that produced, only 25 per cent. remains, which is a very much smaller proportion than that obtained in any former modification of the Clausthal process. In working the 8-tuyered furnace, which at first had a crucible of 4 ft. 8 in. diameter, it was found impossible to blow to the center of the charge, where a pillar of unsmelted material always remained. By shoving the tuyeres toward the center until the diameter of the working hearth was reduced to 1 meter, or 3 ft. 4 in., this difficulty was removed, and this has, therefore, been fixed upon as the standard of a new Piltz, which will have but 4 tuyeres. The other round furnaces do very good work, running through 20 tons of charge (6·7 tons ore) in 24 hours.

At Altenau, 202·6 tons of black copper were treated, producing 288,700 lb. copper, 822·56 lb. silver, and 4,275 tons of sulphuric acid.

From the four establishments at Clausthal, Lautenthal, Altenau and Andreasberg, there were produced in 1871 the following amounts:

43·63	lb. gold,
37,523·0	lb. silver,
7,929·4	tons lead,
47·5	" litharge,
602·0	" refined copper,
5,132·0	" copper vitriol,
427·5	" sulphuric acid,
22·5	" lead paint.

This had a value of $1,497,965.

Francis' Lowell Hydraulics.

Third Edition.

4to. Cloth. $15.00.

LOWELL HYDRAULIC EXPERIMENTS — being a Selection from Experiments on Hydraulic Motors, on the Flow of Water over Weirs, and in Open Canals of Uniform Rectangular Section, made at Lowell, Mass. By J. B. FRANCIS, Civil Engineer. Third edition, revised and enlarged, including many New Experiments on Gauging Water in Open Canals, and on the Flow through Submerged Orifices and Diverging Tubes. With 23 copperplates, beautifully engraved, and about 100 new pages of text.

The work is divided into parts. PART I., on hydraulic motors, includes ninety-two experiments on an improved Fourneyron Turbine Water-Wheel, of about two hundred horse-power, with rules and tables for the construction of similar motors; thirteen experiments on a model of a centre-vent water-wheel of the most simple design, and thirty-nine experiments on a centre-vent water-wheel of about two hundred and thirty horse-power.

PART II. includes seventy-four experiments made for the purpose of determining the form of the formula for computing the flow of water over weirs; nine experiments on the effect of back-water on the flow over weirs; eighty-eight experiments made for the purpose of determining the formula for computing the flow over weirs of regular or standard forms, with several tables of comparisons of the new formula with the results obtained by former experimenters; five experiments on the flow over a dam in which the crest was of the same form as that built by the Essex Company across the Merrimack River at Lawrence, Massachusetts; twenty-one experiments on the effect of observing the depths of water on a weir at different distances from the weir; an extensive series of experiments made for the purpose of determining rules for gauging streams of water in open canals, with tables for facilitating the same; and one hundred and one experiments on the discharge of water through submerged orifices and diverging tubes, the whole being fully illustrated by twenty-three double plates engraved on copper.

In 1855 the proprietors of the Locks and Canals on Merrimack River consented to the publication of the first edition of this work, which contained a selection of the most important hydraulic experiments made at Lowell up to that time. In this edition the principal hydraulic experiments made there, subsequent to 1855, have been added, including the important series above mentioned, for determining rules for the gauging the flow of water in open canals, and the interesting series on the flow through a submerged Venturi's tube, in which a larger flow was obtained than any we find recorded.

Francis on Cast-Iron Pillars.

8vo. Cloth. $2.00.

ON THE STRENGTH OF CAST-IRON PILLARS, with Tables for the use of Engineers, Architects, and Builders. By JAMES B. FRANCIS, Civil Engineer.

Merrill's Iron Truss Bridges.

Second Edition.

4to. Cloth. $5.00.

IRON TRUSS BRIDGES FOR RAILROADS. The Method of Calculating Strains in Trusses, with a careful comparison of the most prominent Trusses, in reference to economy in combination, etc., etc. By Brevet Colonel WILLIAM E. MERRILL, U.S.A., Major Corps of Engineers. Nine lithographed plates of illustrations.

"The work before us is an attempt to give a basis for sound reform in this feature of railroad engineering, by throwing 'additional light upon the method of calculating the maxima strains that can come upon any part of a bridge truss, and upon the manner of proportioning each part, so that it shall be as strong relatively to its own strains as any other part, and so that the entire bridge may be strong enough to sustain several times as great strains as the greatest that can come upon it in actual use.'"—*Scientific American.*

"The author has presented his views in a clear and intelligent manner, and the ingenuity displayed in coloring the figures so as to present certain facts to the eye forms no inappreciable part of the merits of the work. The reduction of the 'formulæ for obtaining the strength, volume, and weight of a cast-iron pillar under a strain of compression,' will be very acceptable to those who have occasion hereafter to make investigations involving these conditions. As a whole, the work has been well done."—*Railroad Gazette, Chicago.*

Humber's Strains in Girders.

18mo. Cloth. $2.50.

A HANDY BOOK FOR THE CALCULATION OF STRAINS IN GIRDERS and Similar Structures, and their Strength, consisting of Formulæ and Corresponding Diagrams, with numerous details for practical application. By WILLIAM HUMBER. Fully illustrated.

Shreve on Bridges and Roofs.

8vo, 87 wood-cut illustrations. Cloth. $5.00.

A TREATISE ON THE STRENGTH OF BRIDGES AND ROOFS—comprising the determination of Algebraic formulas for Strains in Horizontal, Inclined or Rafter, Triangular, Bowstring, Lenticular and other Trusses, from fixed and moving loads, with practical applications and examples, for the use of Students and Engineers. By SAMUEL H. SHREVE, A.M., Civil Engineer.

The rules for the determination of strains given in this work, in the shape of formulas, are deduced from a few well-known mechanical laws, and are not based upon assumed conditions; the processes are given and applications made of the results, so that it is equally valuable as a text-book for the Student and as a manual for the Practical Engineer. Among the examples are the Greithausen Bridge, the Kuilemberg Bridge, a bridge of the Saltash type, and many other compound trusses, whose strains are calculated by methods which are not only free from the use of the higher mathematics, but are as simple and accurate, and as readily applied, as those which are used in proportioning a Warren Girder or other simple truss.

The Kansas City Bridge.

4to. Cloth. $6.00

WITH AN ACCOUNT OF THE REGIMEN OF THE MISSOURI RIVER, and a description of the Methods used for Founding in that River. By O. CHANUTE, Chief Engineer, and GEORGE MORISON, Assistant Engineer. Illustrated with five lithographic views and twelve plates of plans.

Illustrations.

VIEWS.—View of the Kansas City Bridge, August 2, 1869. Lowering Caisson No. 1 into position. Caisson for Pier No. 4 brought into position. View of Foundation Works, Pier No. 4. Pier No. 1.

PLATES.—I. Map showing location of Bridge. II. Water Record—Cross Section of River—Profile of Crossing—Pontoon Protection. III. Water Deadener—Caisson No. 2—Foundation Works, Pier No. 3. IV. Foundation Works, Pier No. 4. V. Foundation Works, Pier No. 4. VI. Caisson No. 5—Sheet Piling at Pier No. 6—Details of Dredges—Pile Shoe—Beton Box. VII. Masonry—Draw Protection—False Works between Piers 3 and 4. VIII. Floating Derricks. IX. General Elevation—176 feet span. X. 248 feet span. XI. Plans of Draw. XII. Strain Diagrams.

Clarke's Quincy Bridge.

4to. Cloth. $7.50.

DESCRIPTION OF THE IRON RAILWAY Bridge across the Mississippi River at Quincy, Illinois. By THOMAS CURTIS CLARKE, Chief Engineer. Illustrated with twenty-one lithographed plans.

Illustrations.

PLATES.—General Plan of Mississippi River at Quincy, showing location of Bridge. II*a*. General Sections of Mississippi River at Quincy, showing location of Bridge. II*b*. General Sections of Mississippi River at Quincy, showing location of Bridge. III. General Sections of Mississippi River at Quincy, showing location of Bridge. IV. Plans of Masonry. V. Diagram of Spans, showing the Dimensions, Arrangement of Panels, etc. VI. Two hundred and fifty feet span, and details. VII. Three hundred and sixty feet Pivot Draw. VIII. Details of three hundred and sixty feet Draw. IX. Ice-Breakers, Foundations of Piers and Abutments, Water Table, and Curve of Deflections. X. Foundations of Pier 2, in Process of Construction. XI. Foundations of Pier 3, and its Protection. XII. Foundations of Pier 3, in Process of Construction, and Steam Dredge. XIII. Foundations of Piers 5 to 18, in Process of Construction. XIV. False Works, showing Process of Handling and Setting Stone. XV. False Works for Raising Iron Work of Superstructure. XVI. Steam Dredge used in Foundations 9 to 18. XVII. Single Bucket Dredge used in Foundations of Bay Piers. XVIII. Saws used for Cutting Piles under water. XIX. Sand Pump and Concrete Box. XX Masonry Travelling Crane.

Whipple on Bridge Building.

8vo, Illustrated. Cloth. $4.00.

AN ELEMENTARY AND PRACTICAL TREATISE ON BRIDGE BUILDING. An enlarged and improved edition of the Author's original work. By S. WHIPPLE, C. E., Inventor of the Whipple Bridges, &c.

The design has been to develop from Fundamental Principles a system easy of comprehension, and such as to enable the attentive reader and student to judge understandingly for himself, as to the relative merits of different plans and combinations, and to adopt for use such as may be most suitable for the cases he may have to deal with.

It is hoped the work may prove an appropriate Text-Book upon the subject treated of, for the Engineering Student, and a useful manual for the Practicing Engineer and Bridge Builder.

Stoney on Strains.

New and Revised Edition, with numerous illustrations.

Royal 8vo, 664 pp. Cloth. $15.00.

THE THEORY OF STRAINS IN GIRDERS and Similar Structures, with Observations on the Application of Theory to Practice, and Tables of Strength and other Properties of Materials. By BINDON B. STONEY, B. A.

Roebling's Bridges.

Imperial folio. Cloth. $25.00.

LONG AND SHORT SPAN RAILWAY BRIDGES. By JOHN A. ROEBLING, C. E. Illustrated with large copperplate engravings of plans and views.

List of Plates

1. Parabolic Truss Railway Bridge. 2, 3, 4, 5, 6. Details of Parabolic Truss, with centre span 500 feet in the clear. 7. Plan and View of a Bridge over the Mississippi River, at St. Louis, for railway and common travel. 8, 9, 10, 11, 12. Details and View of St. Louis Bridge. 13. Railroad Bridge over the Ohio.

Diedrichs' Theory of Strains.

8vo. Cloth. $5.00.

A Compendium for the Calculation and Construction of Bridges, Roofs, and Cranes, with the Application of Trigonometrical Notes. Containing the most comprehensive information in regard to the Resulting Strains for a permanent Load, as also for a combined (Permanent and Rolling) Load. In two sections adapted to the requirements of the present time. By JOHN DIEDRICHS. Illustrated by numerous plates and diagrams.

"The want of a compact, universal and popular treatise on the Construction of Roofs and Bridges—especially one treating of the influence of a variable load—and the unsatisfactory essays of different authors on the subject, induced me to prepare this work."

Whilden's Strength of Materials.

12mo. Cloth. $2.00.

ON THE STRENGTH OF MATERIALS used in Engineering Construction. By J. K. WHILDEN.

Campin on Iron Roofs.

Large 8vo. Cloth. $3.00.

ON THE CONSTRUCTION OF IRON ROOFS. A Theoretical and Practical Treatise. By FRANCIS CAMPIN. With wood-cuts and plates of Roofs lately executed.

"The mathematical formulas are of an elementary kind, and the process admits of an easy extension so as to embrace the prominent varieties of iron truss bridges. The treatise, though of a practical scientific character, may be easily mastered by any one familiar with elementary mechanics and plane trigonometry."

Holley's Railway Practice.

1 vol. folio. Cloth. $12.00.

AMERICAN AND EUROPEAN RAILWAY PRACTICE, in the Economical Generation of Steam, including the materials and construction of Coal-burning Boilers, Combustion, the Variable Blast, Vaporization, Circulation, Super-heating, Supplying and Heating Feed-water, &c., and the adaptation of Wood and Coke-burning Engines to Coal-burning; and in Permanent Way, including Road-bed, Sleepers, Rails, Joint Fastenings, Street Railways, &c., &c. By ALEXANDER L. HOLLEY, B. P. With 77 lithographed plates.

"This is an elaborate treatise by one of our ablest civil engineers, on the construction and use of locomotives, with a few chapters on the building of Railroads. * * * All these subjects are treated by the author, who is a first-class railroad engineer, in both an intelligent and intelligible manner. The facts and ideas are well arranged, and presented in a clear and simple style, accompanied by beautiful engravings, and we presume the work will be regarded as indispensable by all who are interested in a knowledge of the construction of railroads and rolling stock, or the working of locomotives."—*Scientific American.*

Henrici's Skeleton Structures.

8vo. Cloth. $3.00.

SKELETON STRUCTURES, especially in their Application to the building of Steel and Iron Bridges. By OLAUS HENRICI. With folding plates and diagrams.

By presenting these general examinations on Skeleton Structures, with particular application for Suspended Bridges, to Engineers, I venture to express the hope that they will receive these theoretical results with some confidence, even although an opportunity is wanting to compare them with practical results. O. H.

Useful Information for Railway Men.

Pocket form. Morocco, gilt, $2.00.

Compiled by W. G. HAMILTON, Engineer. Fifth edition, revised and enlarged. 570 pages.

"It embodies many valuable formulæ and recipes useful for railway men, and, indeed, for almost every class of persons in the world. The 'information' comprises some valuable formulæ and rules for the construction of boilers and engines, masonry, properties of steel and iron, and the strength of materials generally."—*Railroad Gazette, Chicago.*

Brooklyn Water Works.

1 vol. folio. Cloth. $20.00.

A DESCRIPTIVE ACCOUNT OF THE CONSTRUCTION OF THE WORKS, and also Reports on the Brooklyn, Hartford, Belleville, and Cambridge Pumping Engines. Prepared and printed by order of the Board of Water Commissioners. With 59 illustrations.

CONTENTS.—Supply Ponds—The Conduit—Ridgewood Engine House and Pump Well—Ridgewood Engines—Force Mains—Ridgewood Reservoir—Pipe Distribution—Mount Prospect Reservoir—Mount Prospect Engine House and Engine—Drainage Grounds—Sewerage Works—Appendix.

Kirkwood on Filtration.

4to. Cloth. $15.00.

REPORT ON THE FILTRATION OF RIVER WATERS, for the Supply of Cities, as practised in Europe, made to the Board of Water Commissioners of the City of St. Louis. By JAMES P. KIRKWOOD. Illustrated by 30 double-plate engravings.

CONTENTS.—Report on Filtration—London Works, General—Chelsea Water Works and Filters—Lambeth Water Works and Filters—Southwark and Vauxhall Water Works and Filters—Grand Junction Water Works and Filters—West Middlesex Water Works and Filters—New River Water Works and Filters—East London Water Works and Filters—Leicester Water Works and Filters—York Water Works and Filters—Liverpool Water Works and Filters—Edinburgh Water Works and Filters—Dublin Water Works and Filters—Perth Water Works and Filtering Gallery—Berlin Water Works and Filters—Hamburg Water Works and Reservoirs—Altona Water Works and Filters—Tours Water Works and Filtering Canal—Angers Water Works and Filtering Galleries—Nantes Water Works and Filters—Lyons Water Works and Filtering Galleries—Toulouse Water Works and Filtering Galleries—Marseilles Water Works and Filters—Genoa Water Works and Filtering Galleries—Leghorn Water Works and Cisterns—Wakefield Water Works and Filters—Appendix.

Tunner on Roll-Turning.

1 vol. 8vo. and 1 vol. plates. $10.00.

A TREATISE ON ROLL-TURNING FOR THE MANUFACTURE OF IRON. By PETER TUNNER. Translated and adapted. By JOHN B. PEARSE, of the Pennsylvania Steel Works. With numerous wood-cuts, 8vo., together with a folio atlas of 10 lithographed plates of Rolls, Measurements, &c.

"We commend this book as a clear, elaborate, and practical treatise upon the department of iron manufacturing operations to which it is devoted. The writer states in his preface, that for twenty-five years he has felt the necessity of such a work, and has evidently brought to its preparation the fruits of experience, a painstaking regard for accuracy of statement, and a desire to furnish information in a style readily understood. The book should be in the hands of every one interested, either in the general practice of mechanical engineering, or the special branch of manufacturing operations to which the work relates."—*American Artisan.*

Glynn on the Power of Water.

12mo. Cloth. $1.00.

A TREATISE ON THE POWER OF WATER, as applied to drive Flour Mills, and to give motion to Turbines and other Hydrostatic Engines. By JOSEPH GLYNN, F.R. S. Third edition, revised and enlarged, with numerous illustrations.

Hewson on Embankments.

8vo. Cloth. $2.00.

PRINCIPLES AND PRACTICE OF EMBANKING LANDS from River Floods, as applied to the Levees of the Mississippi. By WILLIAM HEWSON, Civil Engineer.

"This is a valuable treatise on the principles and practice of embanking lands from river floods, as applied to the Levees of the Mississippi, by a highly intelligent and experienced engineer. The author says it is a first attempt to reduce to order and to rule the design, execution, and measurement of the Levees of the Mississippi. It is a most useful and needed contribution to scientific literature.—*Philadelphia Evening Journal.*

Grüner on Steel.

8vo. Cloth. $3.50.

THE MANUFACTURE OF STEEL. By M. L. GRUNER, translated from the French. By Lenox Smith, A. M., E. M., with an appendix on the Bessemer Process in the United States, by the translator. Illustrated by lithographed drawings and wood-cuts.

"The purpose of the work is to present a careful, elaborate, and at the same time practical examination into the physical properties of steel, as well as a description of the new processes and mechanical appliances for its manufacture. The information which it contains, gathered from many trustworthy sources, will be found of much value to the American steel manufacturer, who may thus acquaint himself with the results of careful and elaborate experiments in other countries, and better prepare himself for successful competition in this important industry with foreign makers. The fact that this volume is from the pen of one of the ablest metallurgists of the present day, cannot fail, we think, to secure for it a favorable consideration.—*Iron Age.*

Bauerman on Iron.

12mo. Cloth. $2.00.

TREATISE ON THE METALLURGY OF IRON. Containing outlines of the History of Iron Manufacture, methods of Assay, and analysis of Iron Ores, processes of manufacture of Iron and Steel, etc., etc. By H. BAUERMAN. First American edition. Revised and enlarged, with an appendix on the Martin Process for making Steel, from the report of Abram S. Hewitt. Illustrated with numerous wood engravings.

"This is an important addition to the stock of technical works published in this country. It embodies the latest facts, discoveries, and processes connected with the manufacture of iron and steel, and should be in the hands of every person interested in the subject, as well as in all technical and scientific libraries."—*Scientific American.*

Link and Valve Motions, by W. S. Auchincloss.

8vo. Cloth. $3.00.

APPLICATION OF THE SLIDE VALVE and Link Motion to Stationary, Portable, Locomotive and Marine Engines, with new and simple methods for proportioning the parts. By WILLIAM S. AUCHINCLOSS, Civil and Mechanical Engineer. Designed as a hand-book for Mechanical Engineers, Master Mechanics, Draughtsmen and Students of Steam Engineering. All dimensions of the valve are found with the greatest ease by means of a Printed Scale, and proportions of the link determined *without* the assistance of a model. Illustrated by 37 wood-cuts and 21 lithographic plates, together with a copperplate engraving of the Travel Scale.

All the matters we have mentioned are treated with a clearness and absence of unnecessary verbiage which renders the work a peculiarly valuable one. The Travel Scale only requires to be known to be appreciated. Mr. A. writes so ably on his subject, we wish he had written more. *London Engineering.*

We have never opened a work relating to steam which seemed to us better calculated to give an intelligent mind a clear understanding of the department it discusses.—*Scientific American.*

Slide Valve by Eccentrics, by Prof. C. W. MacCord.

4to. Illustrated. Cloth, $4.00.

A PRACTICAL TREATISE ON THE SLIDE VALVE BY ECCENTRICS, examining by methods, the action of the Eccentric upon the Slide Valve, and explaining the practical processes of laying out the movements, adapting the valve for its various duties in the steam-engine. For the use of Engineers, Draughtsmen, Machinists, and Students of valve motions in general. By C. W. MacCord, A. M., Professor of Mechanical Drawing, Stevens' Institute of Technology, Hoboken, N J.

Stillman's Steam-Engine Indicator.

12mo. Cloth. $1.00.

THE STEAM-ENGINE INDICATOR, and the Improved Manometer Steam and Vacuum Gauges; their utility and application By Paul Stillman. New edition.

Bacon's Steam-Engine Indicator.

12mo. Cloth. $1.00. Mor. $1.50.

A TREATISE ON THE RICHARDS STEAM-ENGINE INDICATOR, with directions for its use. By Charles T. Porter. Revised, with notes and large additions as developed by American Practice, with an Appendix containing useful formulæ and rules for Engineers. By F. W. Bacon, M. E., Member of the American Society of Civil Engineers. Illustrated.

In this work, Mr. Porter's book has been taken as the basis, but Mr. Bacon has adapted it to American Practice, and has conferred a great boon on American Engineers.—*Artisan.*

Bartol on Marine Boilers.

8vo. Cloth. $1.50.

TREATISE ON THE MARINE BOILERS OF THE UNITED STATES. By H. B. Bartol. Illustrated.

Gillmore's Limes and Cements.

Fourth Edition. Revised and Enlargd.

8vo. Cloth. $4.00.

PRACTICAL TREATISE ON LIMES, HYDRAULIC CEMENTS, AND MORTARS. Papers on Practical Engineering, U. S. Engineer Department, No. 9, containing Reports of numerous experiments conducted in New York City, during the years 1858 to 1861, inclusive. By Q. A. GILLMORE, Brig-General U. S. Volunteers, and Major U. S. Corps of Engineers. With numerous illustrations.

"This work contains a record of certain experiments and researches made under the authority of the Engineer Bureau of the War Department from 1858 to 1861, upon the various hydraulic cements of the United States, and the materials for their manufacture. The experiments were carefully made, and are well reported and compiled.'—*Journal Franklin Institute.*

Gillmore's Coignet Beton.

8vo. Cloth. $2.50.

COIGNET BETON AND OTHER ARTIFICIAL STONE. By Q. A. GILLMORE. 9 Plates, Views, etc.

This work describes with considerable minuteness of detail the several kinds of artificial stone in most general use in Europe and now beginning to be introduced in the United States, discusses their properties, relative merits, and cost, and describes the materials of which they are composed. . . . . The subject is one of special and growing interest, and we commend the work, embodying as it does the matured opinions of an experienced engineer and expert.

Williamson's Practical Tables.

4to. Flexible Cloth. $2.50.

PRACTICAL TABLES IN METEOROLOGY AND HYPSOMETRY, in connection with the use of the Barometer. By Col. R. S. WILLIAMSOM, U. S. A.

Williamson on the Barometer.

4to. Cloth. $15.00.

ON THE USE OF THE BAROMETER ON SURVEYS AND RECONNAISSANCES. Part I. Meteorology in its Connection with Hypsometry. Part II. Barometric Hypsometry. By R. S. WILLIAMSON, Bvt. Lieut.-Col. U. S. A., Major Corps of Engineers. With Illustrative Tables and Engravings. Paper No. 15, Professional Papers, Corps of Engineers.

"SAN FRANCISCO, CAL., *Feb.* 27, 1867.

"Gen. A. A. HUMPHREYS, Chief of Engineers, U. S. Army:

"GENERAL,—I have the honor to submit to you, in the following pages, the results of my investigations in meteorology and hypsometry, made with the view of ascertaining how far the barometer can be used as a reliable instrument for determining altitudes on extended lines of survey and reconnaissances. These investigations have occupied the leisure permitted me from my professional duties during the last ten years, and I hope the results will be deemed of sufficient value to have a place assigned them among the printed professional papers of the United States Corps of Engineers.

"Very respectfully, your obedient servant,

"R. S. WILLIAMSON,

"Bvt. Lt.-Col. U. S. A., Major Corps of U. S. Engineers."

Von Cotta's Ore Deposits.

8vo. Cloth. $4.00.

TREATISE ON ORE DEPOSITS. By BERNHARD VON COTTA, Professor of Geology in the Royal School of Mines, Freidberg, Saxony. Translated from the second German edition, by FREDERICK PRIME, Jr., Mining Engineer, and revised by the author, with numerous illustrations.

"Prof. Von Cotta of the Freiberg School of Mines, is the author of the best modern treatise on ore deposits, and we are heartily glad that this admirable work has been translated and published in this country. The translator, Mr. Frederick Prime, Jr., a graduate of Freiberg, has had in his work the great advantage of a revision by the author himself, who declares in a prefatory note that this may be considered as a new edition (the third) of his own book.

"It is a timely and welcome contribution to the literature of mining in this country, and we are grateful to the translator for his enterprise and good judgment in undertaking its preparation; while we recognize with equal cordiality the liberality of the author in granting both permission and assistance."—*Extract from Review in Engineering and Mining Journal.*

Plattner's Blow-Pipe Analysis.

Second edition. Revised. 8vo. Cloth. $7.50.

PLATTNER'S MANUAL OF QUALITATIVE AND QUANTITATIVE ANALYSIS WITH THE BLOW-PIPE. From the last German edition Revised and enlarged. By Prof. TH. RICHTER, of the Royal Saxon Mining Academy. Translated by Prof. H. B. CORNWALL, Assistant in the Columbia School of Mines, New York; assisted by JOHN H. CASWELL. Illustrated with eighty-seven wood-cuts and one Lithographic Plate. 560 pages.

"Plattner's celebrated work has long been recognized as the only complete book on Blow-Pipe Analysis. The fourth German edition, edited by Prof. Richter, fully sustains the reputation which the earlier editions acquired during the lifetime of the author, and it is a source of great satisfaction to us to know that Prof. Richter has co-operated with the translator in issuing the American edition of the work, which is in fact a fifth edition of the original work, being far more complete than the last German edition."—*Silliman's Journal.*

There is nothing so complete to be found in the English language. Plattner's book is not a mere pocket edition; it is intended as a comprehensive guide to all that is at present known on the blow-pipe, and as such is really indispensable to teachers and advanced pupils.

"Mr. Cornwall's edition is something more than a translation, as it contains many corrections, emendations and additions not to be found in the original. It is a decided improvement on the work in its German dress."—*Journal of Applied Chemistry.*

Egleston's Mineralogy.

8vo. Illustrated with 34 Lithographic Plates. Cloth. $4.50.

LECTURES ON DESCRIPTIVE MINERALOGY, Delivered at the School of Mines, Columbia College. BY PROFESSOR T. EGLESTON.

These lectures are what their title indicates, the lectures on Mineralogy delivered at the School of Mines of Columbia College. They have been printed for the students, in order that more time might be given to the various methods of examining and determining minerals. The second part has only been printed. The first part, comprising crystallography and physical mineralogy, will be printed at some future time.

Pynchon's Chemical Physics.

New Edition. Revised and Enlarged.

Crown 8vo. Cloth. $3.00.

INTRODUCTION TO CHEMICAL PHYSICS, Designed for the Use of Academies, Colleges, and High Schools. Illustrated with numerous engravings, and containing copious experiments with directions for preparing them. By THOMAS RUGGLES PYNCHON, M.A., Professor of Chemistry and the Natural Sciences, Trinity College, Hartford.

Hitherto, no work suitable for general use, treating of all these subjects within the limits of a single volume, could be found; consequently the attention they have received has not been at all proportionate to their importance. It is believed that a book containing so much valuable information within so small a compass, cannot fail to meet with a ready sale among all intelligent persons, while Professional men, Physicians, Medical Students, Photographers, Telegraphers, Engineers, and Artisans generally, will find it specially valuable, if not nearly indispensable, as a book of reference.

"We strongly recommend this able treatise to our readers as the first work ever published on the subject free from perplexing technicalities. In style it is pure, in description graphic, and its typographical appearance is artistic. It is altogether a most excellent work."—*Eclectic Medical Journal.*

"It treats fully of Photography, Telegraphy, Steam Engines, and the various applications of Electricity. In short, it is a carefully prepared volume, abreast with the latest scientific discoveries and inventions."—*Hartford Courant.*

Plympton's Blow-Pipe Analysis.

12mo. Cloth. $2.00.

THE BLOW-PIPE: A System of Instruction in its practical use being a graduated course of Analysis for the use of students, and all those engaged in the Examination of Metallic Combinations. Second edition, with an appendix and a copious index. By GEORGE W. PLYMPTON, of the Polytechnic Institute, Brooklyn.

"This manual probably has no superior in the English language as a textbook for beginners, or as a guide to the student working without a teacher. To the latter many illustrations of the utensils and apparatus required in using the blow-pipe, as well as the fully illustrated description of the blow-pipe flame, will be especially serviceable."—*New York Teacher.*

Ure's Dictionary.

Sixth Edition.

London, 1872.

3 vols. 8vo. Cloth, $25.00. Half Russia, $37.50.

DICTIONARY OF ARTS, MANUFACTURES, AND MINES. By ANDREW URE, M.D. Sixth edition. Edited by ROBERT HUNT, F.R.S., greatly enlarged and rewritten.

Brande and Cox's Dictionary.

New Edition.

London, 1872.

3 vols. 8vo. Cloth, $20.00. Half Morocco, $27.50.

A Dictionary of Science, Literature, and Art. Edited by W. T. BRANDE and Rev. GEO. W. COX. New and enlarged edition.

Watt's Dictionary of Chemistry.

Supplementary Volume.

8vo. Cloth. $9.00.

This volume brings the Record of Chemical Discovery down to the end of the year 1869, including also several additions to, and corrections of, former results which have appeared in 1870 and 1871.

*** Complete Sets of the Work, New and Revised edition, including above supplement. 6 vols. 8vo. Cloth. $62.00.

Rammelsberg's Chemical Analysis.

8vo. Cloth. $2.25.

GUIDE TO A COURSE OF QUANTITATIVE CHEMICAL ANALYSIS, ESPECIALLY OF MINERALS AND FURNACE PRODUCTS. Illustrated by Examples. By C. F. RAMMELSBERG. Translated by J. TOWLER, M.D.

This work has been translated, and is now published expressly for those students in chemistry whose time and other studies in colleges do not permit them to enter upon the more elaborate and expensive treatises of Fresenius and others. It is the condensed labor of a master in chemistry and of a practical analyst.

Eliot and Storer's Qualitative Chemical Analysis.

New Edition, Revised.

12mo. Illustrated. Cloth. $1.50.

A COMPENDIOUS MANUAL OF QUALITATIVE CHEMICAL ANALYSIS. By CHARLES W. ELIOT and FRANK H. STORER. Revised with the Coöperation of the Authors, by WILLIAM RIPLEY NICHOLS, Professor of Chemistry in the Massachusetts Institute of Technology.

"This Manual has great merits as a practical introduction to the science and the art of which it treats. It contains enough of the theory and practice of qualitative analysis, "in the wet way," to bring out all the reasoning involved in the science, and to present clearly to the student the most approved methods of the art. It is specially adapted for exercises and experiments in the laboratory; and yet its classifications and manner of treatment are so systematic and logical throughout, as to adapt it in a high degree to that higher class of students generally who desire an accurate knowledge of the practical methods of arriving at scientific facts."—*Lutheran Observer.*

"We wish every academical class in the land could have the benefit of the fifty exercises of two hours each necessary to master this book. Chemistry would cease to be a mere matter of memory, and become a pleasant experimental and intellectual recreation. We heartily commend this little volume to the notice of those teachers who believe in using the sciences as means of mental discipline."—*College Courant.*

Craig's Decimal System.

Square 32mo. Limp. 50c.

WEIGHTS AND MEASURES. An Account of the Decimal System, with Tables of Conversion for Commercial and Scientific Uses. By B. F. CRAIG, M. D.

"The most lucid, accurate, and useful of all the hand-books on this subject that we have yet seen. It gives forty-seven tables of comparison between the English and French denominations of length, area, capacity, weight, and the Centigrade and Fahrenheit thermometers, with clear instructions how to use them; and to this practical portion, which helps to make the transition as easy as possible, is prefixed a scientific explanation of the errors in the metric system, and how they may be corrected in the laboratory."—*Nation.*

Nugent on Optics.

12mo. Cloth. $2.00

TREATISE ON OPTICS; or, Light and Sight, theoretically and practically treated; with the application to Fine Art and Industrial Pursuits. By E. NUGENT. With one hundred and three illustrations.

"This book is of a practical rather than a theoretical kind, and is designed to afford accurate and complete information to all interested in applications of the science."—*Round Table.*

Barnard's Metric System.

8vo. Brown cloth. $3.00.

THE METRIC SYSTEM OF WEIGHTS AND MEASURES. An Address delivered before the Convocation of the University of the State of New York, at Albany, August, 1871. By FREDERICK A. P. BARNARD, President of Columbia College, New York City. Second edition from the Revised edition printed for the Trustees of Columbia College. Tinted paper.

"It is the best summary of the arguments in favor of the metric weights and measures with which we are acquainted, not only because it contains in small space the leading facts of the case, but because it puts the advocacy of that system on the only tenable grounds, namely, the great convenience of a decimal notation of weight and measure as well as money, the value of international uniformity in the matter, and the fact that this metric system is adopted and in general use by the majority of civilized nations."—*The Nation.*

The Young Mechanic.

Illustrated. 12mo. Cloth. $1.75.

THE YOUNG MECHANIC. Containing directions for the use of all kinds of tools, and for the construction of steam engines and mechanical models, including the Art of Turning in Wood and Metal. By the author of "The Lathe and its Uses," etc From the English edition, with corrections.

Harrison's Mechanic's Tool-Book.

12mo. Cloth. $1.50.

MECHANIC'S TOOL BOOK, with practical rules and suggestions, for the use of Machinists, Iron Workers, and others. By W. B. HARRISON, Associate Editor of the "American Artisan." Illustrated with 44 engravings.

"This work is specially adapted to meet the wants of Machinists and workers in iron generally. It is made up of the work-day experience of an intelligent and ingenious mechanic, who had the faculty of adapting tools to various purposes. The practicability of his plans and suggestions are made apparent even to the unpractised eye by a series of well-executed wood engravings."—*Philadelphia Inquirer.*

Pope's Modern Practice of the Electric Telegraph.

Seventh edition. 8vo. Cloth $2.00.

A Hand-book for Electricians and Operators. By FRANK L. POPE. Seventh edition. Revised and enlarged, and fully illustrated.

Extract from Letter of Prof. Morse.

"I have had time only cursorily to examine its contents, but this examination has resulted in great gratification, especially at the fairness and unprejudiced tone of your whole work.

"Your illustrated diagrams are admirable and beautifully executed.

"I think all your instructions in the use of the telegraph apparatus judicious and correct, and I most cordially wish you success."

Extract from Letter of Prof. G. W. Hough, of the Dudley Observatory.

"There is no other work of this kind in the English language that contains in so small a compass so much practical information in the application of galvanic electricity to telegraphy. It should be in the hands of every one interested in telegraphy, or the use of Batteries for other purposes."

Morse's Telegraphic Apparatus.

Illustrated. 8vo. Cloth. $2.00.

EXAMINATION OF THE TELEGRAPHIC APPARATUS AND THE PROCESSES IN TELEGAPHY. By SAMUEL F. B. MORSE, LL.D., United States Commissioner Paris Universal Exposition, 1867.

Sabine's History of the Telegraph.

12mo. Cloth. $1.25.

HISTORY AND PROGRESS OF THE ELECTRIC TELEGRAPH, with Descriptions of some of the Apparatus. By Robert Sabine, C. E. Second edition, with additions.

Contents.—I. Early Observations of Electrical Phenomena. II. Telegraphs by Frictional Electricity. III. Telegraphs by Voltaic Electricity. IV. Telegraphs by Electro-Magnetism and Magneto-Electricity. V. Telegraphs now in use. VI. Overhead Lines. VII. Submarine Telegraph Lines. VIII. Underground Telegraphs. IX. Atmospheric Electricity.

Shaffner's Telegraph Manual.

8vo. Cloth. $6.50.

A COMPLETE HISTORY AND DESCRIPTION OF THE SEMAPHORIC, ELECTRIC, AND MAGNETIC TELEGRAPHS OF EUROPE, ASIA, AFRICA, AND AMERICA, with 625 illustrations. By Tal. P. Shaffner, of Kentucky. New edition.

Culley's Hand-Book of Telegraphy.

8vo. Cloth. $5.00.

A HAND-BOOK OF PRACTICAL TELEGRAPHY. By R. S. Culley, Engineer to the Electric and International Telegraph Company. Fourth edition, revised and enlarged.

Foster's Submarine Blasting.

4to. Cloth. $3.50.

SUBMARINE BLASTING in Boston Harbor, Massachusetts—Removal of Tower and Corwin Rocks. By John G. Foster, Lieutenant-Colonel of Engineers, and Brevet Major-General, U. S. Army. Illustrated with seven plates.

List of Plates.—1. Sketch of the Narrows, Boston Harbor. 2. Townsend's Submarine Drilling Machine, and Working Vessel attending. 3. Submarine Drilling Machine employed. 4. Details of Drilling Machine employed. 5. Cartridges and Tamping used. 6. Fuses and Insulated Wires used. 7. Portable Friction Battery used.

Barnes' Submarine Warfare.

8vo. Cloth. $5.00.

SUBMARINE WARFARE, DEFENSIVE AND OFFENSIVE. Comprising a full and complete History of the Invention of the Torpedo, its employment in War and results of its use. Descriptions of the various forms of Torpedoes, Submarine Batteries and Torpedo Boats actually used in War. Methods of Ignition by Machinery, Contact Fuzes, and Electricity, and a full account of experiments made to determine the Explosive Force of Gunpowder under Water. Also a discussion of the Offensive Torpedo system, its effect upon Iron-Clad Ship systems, and influence upon Future Naval Wars. By Lieut.-Commander JOHN S. BARNES, U. S. N. With twenty lithographic plates and many wood-cuts.

"A book important to military men, and especially so to engineers and artillerists. It consists of an examination of the various offensive and defensive engines that have been contrived for submarine hostilities, including a discussion of the torpedo system, its effects upon iron-clad ship-systems, and its probable influence upon future naval wars. Plates of a valuable character accompany the treatise, which affords a useful history of the momentous subject it discusses. A great deal of useful information is collected in its pages, especially concerning the inventions of SCHOLL and VERDU, and of JONES' and HUNT'S batteries, as well as of other similar machines, and the use in submarine operations of gun-cotton and nitro-glycerine."—*N. Y. Times.*

Randall's Quartz Operator's Hand-Book.

12mo. Cloth. $2.00.

QUARTZ OPERATOR'S HAND-BOOK. By P. M. RANDALL. New edition, revised and enlarged. Fully illustrated.

The object of this work has been to present a clear and comprehensive exposition of mineral veins, and the means and modes chiefly employed for the mining and working of their ores—more especially those containing gold and silver.

Mitchell's Manual of Assaying.

8vo. Cloth. $10.00.

A MANUAL OF PRACTICAL ASSAYING. By JOHN MITCHELL. Third edition. Edited by WILLIAM CROOKES, F.R.S.

In this edition are incorporated all the late important discoveries in Assaying made in this country and abroad, and special care is devoted to the very important Volumetric and Colorimetric Assays, as well as to the Blow-Pipe Assays.

Benét's Chronoscope.

Second Edition.

Illustrated. 4to. Cloth. $3.00.

ELECTRO-BALLISTIC MACHINES, and the Schultz Chronoscope. By Lieutenant-Colonel S. V. BENÉT, Captain of Ordnance, U. S. Army.

CONTENTS.—1. Ballistic Pendulum. 2. Gun Pendulum. 3. Use of Electricity. 4. Navez' Machine. 5. Vignotti's Machine, with Plates. 6. Benton's Electro-Ballistic Pendulum, with Plates. 7. Leur's Tro-Pendulum Machine 8. Schultz's Chronoscope, with two Plates.

Michaelis' Chronograph.

4to. Illustrated. Cloth. $3.00.

THE LE BOULENGÉ CHRONOGRAPH. With three lithographed folding plates of illustrations. By Brevet Captain O E. MICHAELIS, First Lieutenant Ordnance Corps, U. S. Army.

"The excellent monograph of Captain Michaelis enters minutely into the details of construction and management, and gives tables of the times of flight calculated upon a given fall of the chronometer for all distances. Captain Michaelis has done good service in presenting this work to his brother officers, describing, as it does, an instrument which bids fair to be in constant use in our future ballistic experiments.' —*Army and Navy Journal.*

Silversmith's Hand-Book.

Fourth Edition.

Illustrated. 12mo. Cloth. $3.00.

A PRACTICAL HAND-BOOK FOR MINERS, Metallurgists, and Assayers, comprising the most recent improvements in the disintegration, amalgamation, smelting, and parting of the Precious Ores, with a Comprehensive Digest of the Mining Laws. Greatly augmented, revised, and corrected. By JULIUS SILVERSMITH. Fourth edition. Profusely illustrated. 1 vol. 12mo. Cloth. $3.00.

One of the most important features of this work is that in which the metallurgy of the precious metals is treated of. In it the author has endeavored to embody all the processes for the reduction and manipulation of the precious ores heretofore successfully employed in Germany, England, Mexico, and the United States, together with such as have been more recently invented, and not yet fully tested—all of which are profusely illustrated and easy of comprehension.

Simms' Levelling.

8vo. Cloth. $2.50.

A TREATISE ON THE PRINCIPLES AND PRACTICE OF LEVELLING, showing its application to purposes of Railway Engineering and the Construction of Roads, &c. By FREDERICK W. SIMMS, C. E. From the fifth London edition, revised and corrected, with the addition of Mr. Law's Practical Examples for Setting Out Railway Curves. Illustrated with three lithographic plates and numerous wood-cuts.

"One of the most important text-books for the general surveyor, and there is scarcely a question connected with levelling for which a solution would be sought, but that would be satisfactorily answered by consulting this volume." —*Mining Journal.*

"The text-book on levelling in most of our engineering schools and colleges."—*Engineers.*

"The publishers have rendered a substantial service to the profession, especially to the younger members, by bringing out the present edition of Mr. Simms' useful work."—*Engineering.*

Eads' Naval Defences.

4to. Cloth. $5.00.

SYSTEM OF NAVAL DEFENCES. By JAMES B. EADS, C. E. Report to the Honorable Gideon Welles, Secretary of the Navy, February 22, 1868, with ten illustrations.

Stuart's Naval Dry Docks.

Twenty-four engravings on steel.

Fourth Edition.

4to. Cloth. $6.00.

THE NAVAL DRY DOCKS OF THE UNITED STATES. By CHARLES B. STUART. Engineer in Chief of the United States Navy.

List of Illustrations.

Pumping Engine and Pumps—Plan of Dry Dock and Pump-Well—Sections of Dry Dock—Engine House—Iron Floating Gate—Details of Floating Gate—Iron Turning Gate—Plan of Turning Gate—Culvert Gate—Filling Culvert Gates—Engine Bed—Plate, Pumps, and Culvert—Engine House Roof—Floating Sectional Dock—Details of Section, and Plan of Turn-Tables—Plan of Basin and Marine Railways—Plan of Sliding Frame, and Elevation of Pumps—Hydraulic Cylinder—Plan of Gearing for Pumps and End Floats—Perspective View of Dock, Basin, and Railway—Plan of Basin of Portsmouth Dry Dock—Floating Balance Dock—Elevation of Trusses and the Machinery—Perspective View of Balance Dry Dock

---

Free Hand Drawing.

Profusely Illustrated. 18mo. Cloth. 75 cents.

A GUIDE TO ORNAMENTAL, Figure, and Landscape Drawing. By an Art Student.

CONTENTS.—Materials employed in Drawing, and how to use them—On Lines and how to Draw them—On Shading—Concerning lines and shading, with applications of them to simple elementary subjects—Sketches from Nature.

Minifie's Mechanical Drawing.

Eighth Edition.

Royal 8vo. Cloth. $4.00.

A TEXT-BOOK OF GEOMETRICAL DRAWING for the use of Mechanics and Schools, in which the Definitions and Rules of Geometry are familiarly explained; the Practical Problems are arranged, from the most simple to the more complex, and in their description technicalities are avoided as much as possible. With illustrations for Drawing Plans, Sections, and Elevations of Buildings and Machinery; an Introduction to Isometrical Drawing, and an Essay on Linear Perspective and Shadows. Illustrated with over 200 diagrams engraved on steel. By WM. MINIFIE, Architect. Eighth Edition. With an Appendix on the Theory and Application of Colors.

"It is the best work on Drawing that we have ever seen, and is especially a text-book of Geometrical Drawing for the use of Mechanics and Schools. No young Mechanic, such as a Machinist, Engineer, Cabinet-Maker, Millwright, or Carpenter, should be without it."—*Scientific American.*

"One of the most comprehensive works of the kind ever published, and cannot but possess great value to builders. The style is at once elegant and substantial."—*Pennsylvania Inquirer.*

"Whatever is said is rendered perfectly intelligible by remarkably well-executed diagrams on steel, leaving nothing for mere vague supposition; and the addition of an introduction to isometrical drawing, linear perspective, and the projection of shadows, winding up with a useful index to technical terms." —*Glasgow Mechanics' Journal.*

☞ The British Government has authorized the use of this book in their schools of art at Somerset House, London, and throughout the kingdom.

Minifie's Geometrical Drawing.

New Edition. Enlarged.

12mo. Cloth. $2.00.

GEOMETRICAL DRAWING. Abridged from the octavo edition, for the use of Schools. Illustrated with 48 steel plates. New edition, enlarged.

"It is well adapted as a text-book of drawing to be used in our High Schools and Academies where this useful branch of the fine arts has been hitherto too much neglected."—*Boston Journal.*

Bell on Iron Smelting.

8vo. Cloth. $6.00.

CHEMICAL PHENOMENA OF IRON SMELTING. An experimental and practical examination of the circumstances which determine the capacity of the Blast Furnace, the Temperature of the Air, and the Proper Condition of the Materials to be operated upon. By I. LOWTHIAN BELL.

"The reactions which take place in every foot of the blast-furnace have been investigated, and the nature of every step in the process, from the introduction of the raw material into the furnace to the production of the pig iron, has been carefully ascertained, and recorded so fully that any one in the trade can readily avail themselves of the knowledge acquired; and we have no hesitation in saying that the judicious application of such knowledge will do much to facilitate the introduction of arrangements which will still further economize fuel, and at the same time permit of the quality of the resulting metal being maintained, if not improved. The volume is one which no practical pig iron manufacturer can afford to be without if he be desirous of entering upon that competition which nowadays is essential to progress, and in issuing such a work Mr. Bell has entitled himself to the best thanks of every member of the trade."—*London Mining Journal.*

King's Notes on Steam.

Thirteenth Edition.

8vo. Cloth. $2.00.

LESSONS AND PRACTICAL NOTES ON STEAM, the Steam-Engine, Propellers, &c., &c., for Young Engineers, Students, and others. By the late W. R. KING, U. S. N. Revised by Chief-Engineer J. W. KING, U. S. Navy.

"This is one of the best, because eminently plain and practical treatises on the Steam Engine ever published.'—*Philadelphia Press.*

This is the thirteenth edition of a valuable work of the late W. H. King, U. S. N. It contains lessons and practical notes on Steam and the Steam Engine, Propellers, etc. It is calculated to be of great use to young marine engineers, students, and others. The text is illustrated and explained by numerous diagrams and representations of machinery.—*Boston Daily Advertiser.*

Text-book at the U. S. Naval Academy, Annapolis.

Burgh's Modern Marine Engineering.

One thick 4to vol. Cloth. $25.00. Half morocco. $30.00.

MODERN MARINE ENGINEERING, applied to Paddle and Screw Propulsion. Consisting of 36 Colored Plates, 259 Practical Wood-cut Illustrations, and 403 pages of Descriptive Matter, the whole being an exposition of the present practice of the following firms: Messrs. J. Penn & Sons; Messrs. Maudslay, Sons & Field; Messrs. James Watt & Co.; Messrs. J. & G. Rennie; Messrs. R. Napier & Sons; Messrs. J. & W. Dudgeon; Messrs. Ravenhill & Hodgson; Messrs. Humphreys & Tenant; Mr. J. T. Spencer, and Messrs. Forrester & Co. By N. P. Burgh, Engineer.

Principal Contents.—General Arrangements of Engines, 11 examples—General Arrangement of Boilers, 14 examples—General Arrangement of Superheaters, 11 examples—Details of Oscillating Paddle Engines, 34 examples—Condensers for Screw Engines, both Injection and Surface, 20 examples—Details of Screw Engines, 20 examples—Cylinders and Details of Screw Engines, 21 examples—Slide Valves and Details, 7 examples—Slide Valve, Link Motion, 7 examples—Expansion Valves and Gear, 10 examples—Details in General, 30 examples—Screw Propeller and Fittings, 13 examples Engine and Boiler Fittings, 28 examples In relation to the Principles of the Marine Engine and Boiler, 33 examples.

Notices of the Press.

"Every conceivable detail of the Marine Engine, under all its various forms, is profusely, and we must add, admirably illustrated by a multitude of engravings, selected from the best and most modern practice of the first Marine Engineers of the day. The chapter on Condensers is peculiarly valuable. In one word, there is no other work in existence which will bear a moment's comparison with it as an exponent of the skill, talent and practical experience to which is due the splendid reputation enjoyed by many British Marine Engineers."—*Engineer.*

"This very comprehensive work, which was issued in Monthly parts, has just been completed. It contains large and full drawings and copious descriptions of most of the best examples of Modern Marine Engines, and it is a complete theoretical and practical treatise on the subject of Marine Engineering."—*American Artisan.*

This is the only edition of the above work with the beautifully *colored* plates, and it is out of print in England.

Bourne's Treatise on the Steam Engine.

Ninth Edition.

Illustrated. 4to. Cloth. $15.00.

TREATISE ON THE STEAM ENGINE in its various applications to Mines, Mills, Steam Navigation, Railways, and Agriculture, with the theoretical investigations respecting the Motive Power of Heat and the proper Proportions of Steam Engines. Elaborate Tables of the right dimensions of every part, and Practical Instructions for the Manufacture and Management of every species of Engine in actual use. By JOHN BOURNE, being the ninth edition of "A Treatise on the Steam Engine," by the "Artisan Club." Illustrated by thirty-eight plates and five hundred and forty-six wood-cuts.

As Mr. Bourne's work has the great merit of avoiding unsound and immature views, it may safely be consulted by all who are really desirous of acquiring trustworthy information on the subject of which it treats. During the twenty-two years which have elapsed from the issue of the first edition, the improvements introduced in the construction of the steam engine have been both numerous and important, and of these Mr. Bourne has taken care to point out the more prominent, and to furnish the reader with such information as shall enable him readily to judge of their relative value. This edition has been thoroughly modernized, and made to accord with the opinions and practice of the more successful engineers of the present day. All that the book professes to give is given with ability and evident care. The scientific principles which are permanent are admirably explained, and reference is made to many of the more valuable of the recently introduced engines. To express an opinion of the value and utility of such a work as *The Artisan Club's Treatise on the Steam Engine*, which has passed through eight editions already, would be superfluous; but it may be safely stated that the work is worthy the attentive study of all either engaged in the manufacture of steam engines or interested in economizing the use of steam.—*Mining Journal.*

Isherwood's Engineering Precedents.

Two Vols. in One. 8vo. Cloth. $2.50.

ENGINEERING PRECEDENTS FOR STEAM MACHINERY. Arranged in the most practical and useful manner for Engineers. By B. F. ISHERWOOD, Civil Engineer, U. S. Navy. With illustrations.

Ward's Steam for the Million.

New and Revised Edition.

8vo. Cloth. $1.00.

STEAM FOR THE MILLION. A Popular Treatise on Steam and its Application to the Useful Arts, especially to Navigation. By J. H. WARD, Commander U. S. Navy. New and revised edition.

A most excellent work for the young engineer and general reader. Many facts relating to the management of the boiler and engine are set forth with a simplicity of language and perfection of detail that bring the subject home to the reader.—*American Engineer.*

Walker's Screw Propulsion.

8vo. Cloth. 75 cents.

NOTES ON SCREW PROPULSION, its Rise and History. By Capt. W. H. WALKER, U. S. Navy.

Commander Walker's book contains an immense amount of concise practical data, and every item of information recorded fully proves that the various points bearing upon it have been well considered previously to expressing an opinion.—*London Mining Journal.*

Page's Earth's Crust.

18mo. Cloth. 75 cents.

THE EARTH'S CRUST: a Handy Outline of Geology. By DAVID PAGE.

"Such a work as this was much wanted—a work giving in clear and intelligible outline the leading facts of the science, without amplification or irksome details. It is admirable in arrangement, and clear and easy, and, at the same time, forcible in style. It will lead, we hope, to the introduction of Geology into many schools that have neither time nor room for the study of large treatises."—*The Museum.*

Rogers' Geology of Pennsylvania.

3 Vols. 4to, with Portfolio of Maps. Cloth. $30.00.

THE GEOLOGY OF PENNSYLVANIA. A Government Survey. With a general view of the Geology of the United States, Essays on the Coal Formation and its Fossils, and a description of the Coal Fields of North America and Great Britain. By Henry Darwin Rogers, Late State Geologist of Pennsylvania. Splendidly illustrated with Plates and Engravings in the Text.

It certainly should be in every public library throughout the country, and likewise in the possession of all students of Geology. After the final sale of these copies, the work will, of course, become more valuable.

The work for the last five years has been entirely out of the market, but a few copies that remained in the hands of Prof. Rogers, in Scotland, at the time of his death, are now offered to the public, at a price which is even below what it was originally sold for when first published.

Morfit on Pure Fertilizers.

With 28 Illustrative Plates. 8vo. Cloth. $20.00.

A PRACTICAL TREATISE ON PURE FERTILIZERS, and the Chemical Conversion of Rock Guanos, Marlstones, Coprolites, and the Crude Phosphates of Lime and Alumina Generally, into various Valuable Products. By Campbell Morfit, M.D., F.C.S.

Sweet's Report on Coal.

8vo. Cloth. $3.00.

SPECIAL REPORT ON COAL; showing its Distribution, Classification, and Cost delivered over different routes to various points in the State of New York, and the principal cities on the Atlantic Coast. By S. H. Sweet. With maps.

Colburn's Gas Works of London.

12mo. Boards. 60 cents.

GAS WORKS OF LONDON. By Zerah Colburn.

The Useful Metals and their Alloys; Scoffren, Truran, and others.

Fifth Edition.

8vo. Half calf. $3.75.

THE USEFUL METALS AND THEIR ALLOYS, including MINING VENTILATION, MINING JURISPRUDENCE AND METALLURGIC CHEMISTRY employed in the conversion of IRON, COPPER, TIN, ZINC, ANTIMONY, AND LEAD ORES, with their applications to THE INDUSTRIAL ARTS. By JOHN SCOFFREN, WILLIAM TRURAN, WILLIAM CLAY, ROBERT OXLAND, WILLIAM FAIRBAIRN, W. C. AITKIN, and WILLIAM VOSE PICKETT.

Collins' Useful Alloys.

18mo. Flexible. 75 cents.

THE PRIVATE BOOK OF USEFUL ALLOYS and Memoranda for Goldsmiths, Jewellers, etc. By JAMES E. COLLINS

This little book is compiled from notes made by the Author from the papers of one of the largest and most eminent Manufacturing Goldsmiths and Jewellers in this country, and as the firm is now no longer in existence, and the Author is at present engaged in some other undertaking, he now offers to the public the benefit of his experience, and in so doing he begs to state that all the alloys, etc., given in these pages may be confidently relied on as being thoroughly practicable.

The Memoranda and Receipts throughout this book are also compiled from practice, and will no doubt be found useful to the practical jeweller. —*Shirley, July,* 1871.

Joynson's Metals Used in Construction.

12mo. Cloth. 75 cents.

THE METALS USED IN CONSTRUCTION: Iron, Steel, Bessemer Metal, etc., etc. By FRANCIS HERBERT JOYNSON. Illustrated.

"In the interests of practical science, we are bound to notice this work; and to those who wish further information, we should say, buy it; and the outlay, we honestly believe, will be considered well spent." —*Scientific Review.*

Holley's Ordnance and Armor.

493 Engravings. Half Roan, $10.00. Half Russia, $12.00.

A TREATISE ON ORDNANCE AND ARMOR—Embracing Descriptions, Discussions, and Professional Opinions concerning the MATERIAL, FABRICATION, Requirements, Capabilities, and Endurance of European and American Guns, for Naval, Sea Coast, and Iron-clad Warfare, and their RIFLING, PROJECTILES, and BREECH-LOADING; also, Results of Experiments against Armor, from Official Records, with an Appendix referring to Gun-Cotton, Hooped Guns, etc., etc. By ALEXANDER L. HOLLEY, B. P. 948 pages, 493 Engravings, and 147 Tables of Results, etc.

CONTENTS.

Peirce's Analytic Mechanics.

4to. Cloth. $10.00.

SYSTEM OF ANALYTIC MECHANICS. Physical and Celestial Mechanics. By BENJAMIN PEIRCE, Perkins Professor of Astronomy and Mathematics in Harvard University, and Consulting Astronomer of the American Ephemeris and Nautical Almanac. Developed in four systems of Analytic Mechanics, Celestial Mechanics, Potential Physics, and Analytic Morphology.

"I have re-examined the memoirs of the great geometers, and have striven to consolidate their latest researches and their most exalted forms of thought into a consistent and uniform treatise. If I have hereby succeeded in opening to the students of my country a readier access to these choice jewels of intellect; if their brilliancy is not impaired in this attempt to reset them; if, in their own constellation, they illustrate each other, and concentrate a stronger light upon the names of their discoverers, and, still more, if any gem which I may have presumed to add is not wholly lustreless in the collection, I shall feel that my work has not been in vain."—*Extract from the Preface.*

Burt's Key to Solar Compass.

Second Edition.

Pocket Book Form. Tuck. $2.50.

KEY TO THE SOLAR COMPASS, and Surveyor's Companion; comprising all the Rules necessary for use in the field; also, Description of the Linear Surveys and Public Land System of the United States, Notes on the Barometer, Suggestions for an outfit for a Survey of four months, etc., etc., etc. By W. A. BURT, U. S. Deputy Surveyor. Second edition.

Chauvenet's Lunar Distances.

8vo. Cloth. $2.00.

NEW METHOD OF CORRECTING LUNAR DISTANCES, and Improved Method of Finding the Error and Rate of a Chronometer, by equal altitudes. By WM. CHAUVENET, LL.D., Chancellor of Washington University of St. Louis.

Clark's Theoretical Navigation.

8vo. Cloth. $3.00.

THEORETICAL NAVIGATION AND NAUTICAL ASTRONOMY. By LEWIS CLARK, Lieut.-Commander, U. S. Navy. Illustrated with 41 Wood-cuts, including the Vernier.

Prepared for Use at the U. S. Naval Academy.

The Plane Table.

Illustrated. 8vo. Cloth. $2.00.

ITS USES IN TOPOGRAPHICAL SURVEYING. From the Papers of the U. S. Coast Survey.

This work gives a description of the Plane Table employed at the U. S. Coast Survey Office, and the manner of using it.

Pook on Shipbuilding.

8vo. Cloth. $5.00.

METHOD OF COMPARING THE LINES AND DRAUGHTING VESSELS PROPELLED BY SAIL OR STEAM, including a Chapter on Laying off on the Mould-Loft Floor. By SAMUEL M. POOK, Naval Constructor. 1 vol., 8vo. With illustrations. Cloth. $5.00.

Brunnow's Spherical Astronomy.

8vo. Cloth. $6.50.

SPHERICAL ASTRONOMY. By F. BRUNNOW, Ph. Dr. Translated by the Author from the Second German edition.

Van Buren's Formulas.

8vo. Cloth. $2.00.

INVESTIGATIONS OF FORMULAS, for the Strength of the Iron Parts of Steam Machinery. By J. D. VAN BUREN, Jr., C. E. Illustrated.

This is an analytical discussion of the formulæ employed by mechanical engineers in determining the rupturing or crippling pressure in the different parts of a machine. The formulæ are founded upon the principle, that the different parts of a machine should be equally strong, and are developed in reference to the ultimate strength of the material in order to leave the choice of a factor of safety to the judgment of the designer.—*Silliman's Journal.*

Joynson on Machine Gearing.

8vo. Cloth. $2.00.

THE MECHANIC'S AND STUDENT'S GUIDE in the Designing and Construction of General Machine Gearing, as Eccentrics, Screws, Toothed Wheels, etc., and the Drawing of Rectilineal and Curved Surfaces ; with Practical Rules and Details. Edited by FRANCIS HERBERT JOYNSON. Illustrated with 18 folded plates.

"The aim of this work is to be a guide to mechanics in the designing and construction of general machine-gearing. This design it well fulfils, being plainly and sensibly written, and profusely illustrated."—*Sunday Times.*

Barnard's Report, Paris Exposition, 1867.

Illustrated. 8vo. Cloth. $5.00.

REPORT ON MACHINERY AND PROCESSES ON THE INDUSTRIAL ARTS AND APPARATUS OF THE EXACT SCIENCES. By F. A. P. BARNARD, LL.D.—Paris Universal Exposition, 1867.

"We have in this volume the results of Dr. Barnard's study of the Paris Exposition of 1867, in the form of an official Report of the Government. It is the most exhaustive treatise upon modern inventions that has appeared since the Universal Exhibition of 1851, and we doubt if anything equal to it has appeared this century."—*Journal Applied Chemistry.*

Engineering Facts and Figures.

18mo. Cloth. $2.50 per Volume.

AN ANNUAL REGISTER OF PROGRESS IN MECHANICAL ENGINEERING AND CONSTRUCTION, for the Years 1863–64–65–66–67–68. Fully illustrated. 6 volumes.

Each volume sold separately.

Beckwith's Pottery.

8vo. Paper. 60 cents.

OBSERVATIONS ON THE MATERIALS and Manufacture of Terra-Cotta, Stone-Ware, Fire-Brick, Porcelain and Encaustic Tiles, with Remarks on the Products exhibited at the London International Exhibition, 1871. By ARTHUR BECKWITH, Civil Engineer.

"Everything is noticed in this book which comes under the head of Pottery, from fine porcelain to ordinary brick, and aside from the interest which all take in such manufactures, the work will be of considerable value to followers of the ceramic art."—*Evening Mail.*

Dodd's Dictionary of Manufactures, etc.

12mo. Cloth. $2.00.

DICTIONARY OF MANUFACTURES, MINING, MACHINERY, AND THE INDUSTRIAL ARTS. By GEORGE DODD.

This work, a small book on a great subject, treats, in alphabetical arrangement, of those numerous matters which come generally within the range of manufactures and the productive arts. The raw materials—animal, vegetable, and mineral—whence the manufactured products are derived, are succinctly noticed in connection with the processes which they undergo, but not as subjects of natural history. The operations of the Mine and the Mill, the Foundry and the Forge, the Factory and the Workshop, are passed under review. The principal machines and engines, tools and apparatus, concerned in manufacturing processes, are briefly described. The scale on which our chief branches of national industry are conducted, in regard to values and quantities, is indicated in various ways.

Stuart's Civil and Military Engineering of America.

8vo. Illustrated. Cloth. $5.00.

THE CIVIL AND MILITARY ENGINEERS OF AMERICA. By General Charles B. Stuart, Author of "Naval Dry Docks of the United States," etc., etc. Embellished with nine finely executed portraits on steel of eminent engineers, and illustrated by engravings of some of the most important and original works constructed in America.

Containing sketches of the Life and Works of Major Andrew Ellicott, James Geddes (with Portrait), Benjamin Wright (with Portrait), Canvass White (with Portrait), David Stanhope Bates, Nathan S. Roberts, Gridley Bryant (with Portrait), General Joseph G. Swift, Jesse L. Williams (with Portrait), Colonel William McRee, Samuel H. Kneass, Captain John Childe with Portrait), Frederick Harbach, Major David Bates Douglas (with Portrait), Jonathan Knight, Benjamin H. Latrobe (with Portrait), Colonel Charles Ellet, Jr. (with Portrait), Samuel Forrer, William Stuart Watson, John A. Roebling.

Alexander's Dictionary of Weights and Measures.

8vo. Cloth. $3.50.

UNIVERSAL DICTIONARY OF WEIGHTS AND MEASURES, Ancient and Modern, reduced to the standards of the United States of America. By J. H. Alexander. New edition. 1 vol.

"As a standard work of reference, this book should be in every library; it is one which we have long wanted, and it will save much trouble and research."—*Scientific American.*

Gouge on Ventilation.

Third Edition Enlarged.

8vo. Cloth. $2.00.

NEW SYSTEM OF VENTILATION, which has been thoroughly tested under the patronage of many distinguished persons. By Henry A. Gouge, with many illustrations.

Saeltzer's Acoustics.

12mo. Cloth. $2.00.

TREATISE ON ACOUSTICS in Connection with Ventilation. With a new theory based on an important discovery, of facilitating clear and intelligible sound in any building. By ALEXANDER SAELTZER.

"A practical and very sound treatise on a subject of great importance to architects, and one to which there has hitherto been entirly too little attention paid. The author's theory is, that, by bestowing proper care upon the point of Acoustics, the requisite ventilation will be obtained, and *vice versa.*—*Brooklyn Union.*

Myer's Manual of Signals.

New Edition. Enlarged.

12mo. 48 Plates full Roan. $5.00.

MANUAL OF SIGNALS, for the Use of Signal Officers in the Field, and for Military and Naval Students, Military Schools, etc. A new edition, enlarged and illustrated. By Brig.-Gen. ALBERT J. MYER, Chief Signal Officer of the Army, Colonel of the Signal Corps during the War of the Rebellion.

Larrabee's Secret Letter and Telegraph Code.

18mo. Cloth. $1.00.

CIPHER AND SECRET LETTER AND TELEGRAPHIC CODE, with Hogg's Improvements. The most perfect secret Code ever invented or discovered. Impossible to read without the Key. Invaluable for Secret, Military, Naval, and Diplomatic Service, as well as for Brokers, Bankers, and Merchants. By C. S. LARRABEE, the original inventor of the scheme.

Hunt's Designs for Central Park Gateways.

4to. Cloth. $5.00.

DESIGNS FOR THE GATEWAYS OF THE SOUTHERN ENTRANCES TO THE CENTRAL PARK. By RICHARD M. HUNT. With a description of the designs.

Pickert and Metcalf's Art of Graining.

1 vol. 4to. Cloth. $10.00.

THE ART OF GRAINING. How Acquired and How Produced, with description of colors and their application. By CHARLES PICKERT and ABRAHAM METCALF. Beautifully illustrated with 42 tinted plates of the various woods used in interior finishing. Tinted paper.

The authors present here the result of long experience in the practice of this decorative art, and feel confident that they hereby offer to their brother artisans a reliable guide to improvement in the practice of graining.

Portrait Gallery of the War.

60 fine Portraits on Steel. Royal 8vo. Cloth. $6.00.

PORTRAIT GALLERY OF THE WAR, CIVIL, MILITARY AND NAVAL. A Biographical Record. Edited by FRANK MOORE.

One Law in Nature.

12mo. Cloth. $1.50.

ONE LAW IN NATURE. By Capt. H. M. LAZELLE, U. S. A. A New Corpuscular Theory, comprehending Unity of Force, Identity of Matter, and its Multiple Atom Constitution, applied to the Physical Affections or Modes of Energy.

West Point Scrap Book.

69 Engravings and Map. 8vo. Extra Cloth. $5.00.

WEST POINT SCRAP BOOK. Being a Collection of Legends, Stories, Songs, etc., of the U. S. Military Academy. By Lieut. O. E. Wood, U. S. A. Beautifully printed on tinted paper.

"It is the work of several different writers, whose names are withheld from the public, but whose contributions all bear a decided flavor of their origin, preserving the unity of a military education and experience. The volume abounds with personal anecdotes and humorous narratives, seasoned with copious specimens of the students' songs, and presenting a vivid, and doubtless a faithful, exhibition of the peculiar lights and shades of West Point life."—*N. Y. Tribune.*

History of West Point.

Second Edition.

With 36 Illustrations and Maps. 8vo. Extra Cloth. $3.50.

HISTORY OF WEST POINT. Its Military Importance during the American Revolution, and the Origin and Progress of the U. S. Military Academy. By Bvt.-Major E. C. Boynton. 416 pages. Printed on tinted paper.

"Aside from its value as an historical record, the volume under notice is an entertaining guide-book to the Military Academy and its surroundings. We have full details of Cadet life from the day of entrance to that of graduation, together with descriptions of the buildings, grounds and monuments. To the multitude of those who have enjoyed at West Point the combined attractions, this book will give, in its descriptive and illustrated portion, especial pleasure."—*New York Evening Post.*

West Point Life.

Oblong 8vo. 21 full-page Illustrations. Cloth. $2.50.

WEST POINT LIFE. A Poem read before the Dialectic Society of the United States Military Academy. Illustrated with Pen and Ink Sketches. By A Cadet. To which is added the song "Benny Havens, Oh!"

"Summer visitors at West Point will especially enjoy these illustrations; and the poem itself may be regarded as a description of Cadet life, as seen from the inside, by one who appreciates it."—*N. Y. Journal of Commerce.*

Guide to West Point

and the U. S. Military Academy, with Maps and Engravings. 18mo. Blue Cloth. Flexible Covers. $1.00.

www.ingramcontent.com/pod-product-compliance
Lightning Source LLC
LaVergne TN
LVHW021408110826
845150LV00007B/1828

* 9 7 8 1 4 2 5 5 1 1 8 1 4 *